More Memories of
BEDFORD

Dedicated to the memory of Philip Holland 1957 - 2001
Co-founder of True North Books

The publishers would like to thank the following companies for their support in the production of this book

Main Sponsor

Harrison & Rowley Limited

Bedford School

Bedford Modern School

Colpac Limited

Cranfield University

De Montfort University

Hanson Brick

Ilex

W & H Peacock

Supply Chain Planning Limited

First published in Great Britain by True North Books Limited
England HX5 9AE

Copyright © True North Books Limited, 2001

ISBN 1 903204 33 X

Text, design and origination by True North Books Limited
Printed and bound by The Amadeus Press Limited

Introduction

Our experiences all help to shape our lives. Eveything we learn brings about a change in us. Our schools, our parents, friends, and the place we come from are all in the melting pot of our personalities. We absorb something from each and every one of them. When we take out the photographs, we are separating these influences and realising how much a part of us they have become. We relive the moments and time has gone backwards. Thankfully the rose-coloured spectacles through which we see them, wipe away most of the bad memories and leave us, with a tear in our eye, remembering the good old days.

We find ourselves uttering contradictory statements like, 'I wouldn't change a single thing', and 'I wish I could do it again, knowing what I know now!' Bricks and mortar become old friends, their passing mourned as they are lost forever. We wallow in sweet nostalgia. 'They were hard times, but we were happy'. The past is still important because it tells us who we are, and what we are. Go to any reference library today and notice how many people are tracing their family trees. There are books about them on the shelves of any bookshop. Computer programmes are written to help make sense of the information obtained. It gives us strength to know a little more about our roots and ourselves.

Like many towns, Bedford, as its name suggests, grew around the ford across the river. Supposedly there was a settlement here, founded by a Saxon chief, Beda. Later, at the time of the Norman Conquest there was a castle built on the banks of the Great Ouse, but little remains of it now. The river is an extremely peaceful place with many delightful tree-lined walks. Swans, and other water birds, can found there. The river was the 'main highway' navigable to King's Lynn. Now it is very much used for pleasure, rather than commerce, and every year a Regatta is held. The original bridge over the river was replaced in the early 1813, by the elegant Town Bridge. Further down the river is the Suspension Bridge, opened in 1888.

Continued overleaf

Bedford's market in
the 1940s

No one can visit Bedford without realising the influence of a few men to the town's growth and development. John Bunyan was born near the village of Elstow, only a few miles from Bedford.

Bunyan was imprisoned in the County Gaol for refusing to recognise the established church. During his incarceration, he wrote his famous book, 'The Pilgrim's Progress'. John Howard spoke up about the appalling conditions in the gaols and prison ships of the eighteenth century. He was responsible for bringing about many improvements in the penal system. He is remembered by the statue of him, which stands in St Paul's Square. Sir William Harpur, who was once a Lord Mayor of London, endowed Bedford with land, which brought wealth to the town. The Harpur Trust now provides five schools, and was, perhaps, the most significant influence on the town's development for the whole of the nineteenth and much of the twentieth

centuries. Many people have good reason to thank Sir William for the sound education they received. His name and that of his wife, Dame Alice, live on in place names in the town. Bedford people fiercely protected the character of their schools following the Butler Act (1944). Whilst the Bedford people could agree with the principle that 'no child should be debarred by poverty from receiving a suitable education', they knew that they had something special in their schools, which they did not wish to change. Some change, they knew, was inevitable, and Bedford Modern School and Dame Alice Harpur School remained Direct Grant Schools, with at least 25 per cent free places.

Most of our own school days are remembered through the 'not so academic' events that occurred. Can you remember the little boy who brought a note to school saying that he was absent for the last few days because there was a hole in his shoe and

Coronation celebrations getting underway along High Street in 1953

his mother had no money to buy any more? His uncle mended them. For how many was a cobbler's last an essential piece of equipment, kept down in the cellar? How many can still remember how to place the shoe onto the new leather and draw around the shape? How many of us can remember dad or uncle using a knife sharp enough to cut through the hide and carve it to shape?

Bedfordshire is famous for the cottage industry of lace making. There is little doubt that, in the early days of the industry, children were exploited. Their general education was neglected in order that they could produce lace. The 'Point Ground' style of lace, where the background and pattern were worked together, was typical of the lace made in the area. With the increase in the production of machine-made lace, the earnings of the

Bedfordshire lace makers fell, and the skills were at risk of being lost. A few survived because the Bedfordshire lace was too intricate to be successfully copied by machine. The Aragon Lacemakers organised themselves in 1977. They hold regular meetings to share their skills and experience, and perpetuate the art.

Around Bedford have grown various industries, from breweries and iron foundries, to car manufacturers and makers of airships. There has always been a careful attempt to protect that which is worth preserving from the past, without impeding progress. It has always found room in its colleges for students from abroad as well as from other parts of the country, and it was generous in offering protection for the children who were evacuated during the war.

Contents

Street scenes

Many people in Bedford were not too pleased when John Bull the jeweller erected his sign above his shop in the High Street, but he declared that he was well satisfied. The golden bull has now become a famous landmark in the town. The one that we see in this picture, which still stands there to this day overlooking the street, is not the original one, but a copy. Behind the bull there was once a pole onto which was threaded a large golden ball. The ball slowly moved up the pole and dropped at 10am each day. John Bull's successors moved the business into premises in St Peter's, but the bull was left behind and still remains above Allders opticians.

All seems so pleasant and peaceful; an end to the war seemed tantalisingly close. Operation Overlord, as the invasion was code-named, had been successful. Allied troops had landed in Normandy. The Russians had broken the siege of Leningrad. London, however, was experiencing attacks from a terrible weapon called the V2. It was a rocket-powered missile which carried a one tonne warhead. It travelled faster than any aircraft and could not be shot down. The only answer to it was to attack the bases from which it was launched.

The exact date of this picture is not known, but it is a time when you could prop your bicycle against the curb by its pedal, whilst you attended to your shopping, and be sure that it would still be there when you returned. When a cyclist could still ride up the High Street in relaxed comfort. When parking spaces were easy to find in Bedford, and parking meters had not yet been imported from America, no one had thought up the idea of yellow lines on the road, traffic wardens were something for the future, and 'stress' was only experienced by your car's chassis.

The Empire Meat Company building has long since been demolished and here now stands, set back from the road, 'Genesis' and 'Ryman' shops. Numbers 42 and 44 was a butcher and fishmonger. An earlier occupant was Thomas Tokelove Gray, a wine merchant and Mayor of Bedford from 1867 to 1868. The two upper floors were the offices of the architect, John Usher. He designed many buildings in Bedford at that time. His office looked across at Adkins the gunsmith at number 57 (now a fabric shop), which he had designed. It is ornately carved and decorated, the gable flanked by two columns on which sit two white gun-dogs.

Left: During the 1940s members of the armed forces, both British and American, became a common sight in Bedford. The corner of Mill Street and High Street, next to the Cross Keys had been widened in 1937 to accommodate the increasing traffic, much of which was now military. The pedestrians have a lot to learn about road discipline as they cross with no regard for the studded crossing now added for them. Crossings were not to get their stripes until 1951 and the beacons, which are missing in this picture even though they were introduced as early as 1934, began to flash only in 1952. The ladies would join a queue as soon as it formed, even if they were not sure what was for sale. All things were scarce, and housewives took whatever was on offer. Ration books were carefully guarded and the coupons used wisely. In 1941 jam, marmalade and even clothes were added to the list of things that were rationed. Meat, bacon, fats, butter, milk, cheese and eggs had already been rationed in 1940. The Government encouraged everyone to eat potatoes and carrots. Carrots, after all were very good for you. 'They help you to see in the dark!' was the joke. But the government seriously encouraged housewives to, 'Mash them up and add them to pastry, or mash them to make a tasty sandwich filling'.

Below: Is the 'Bobby' on the lookout for the intoxicated painter who laid the white lines in the road? The dog may well have picked up the scent. Traffic was increasing and, police on traffic duty became a common sight. The road markings were seriously needed at this junction of the High Street and Mill Street. Before the advent of 'robotic traffic lights', black and white striped boxes were erected at major junctions where the policeman could stand safely to direct the traffic. With few exceptions, everyone is wearing a hat of some kind. The girl in the foreground would possibly choose a 'cloche hat', when she was dressed to go out on the town. They were very fashionable in the twenties, shaped close to the head and pulled down over the ears. Shorter skirts and more liberal attitudes developed after the first world war. Women had done the work of men and now wished to keep that independence. The pram with the large hood seems strange and impractical compared with the modern lightweight collapsible buggy we know today. They did have other compensations, however, in that it was not likely that the pram would be placed in a bus or car, and they gave a more comfortable ride for the child. They often had ample space to accommodate all the shopping and were quite sturdy enough for a shopping bag to be hung from the handle without the possible risk of the pram tilting over.

Above: All who owned a television set, when ITV first began to broadcast, will have that jingle running through their brains the moment their eyes focus on the John Collier shop. It's happened hasn't it? The TV jingle is going through your mind, 'John Collier, John Collier the window to watch'! The 'Montague' has disappeared from 'Burton' tailoring. John Collier was once the 'fifty shilling tailors', who made affordable suits primarily for ex-servicemen, and are now only a few yards further down the road from their rivals. In the middle, benefiting, no doubt from trade from the customers of both outfitters, is Hilton's shoe shop. Cameras are on sale at Vines. The owners could not imagine the changes that would face their trade over the next few years. Computers, digital cameras, are to come, and, one development which is to take away the telephone boxes, the mobile 'phone. No one could have foreseen a culture in which mobile 'phones are pressed to ears and minds are somewhere else, leaving shop windows unnoticed, let alone 'watched'. The snow lingers, making conditions unpleasant for pedestrians and motorists. Brakes were not so efficient and motorists had to anticipate further in advance. The crosshatched markings, of the kind seen here at the junction, were first seen on London's streets in1964. Their aim was to prevent traffic from blocking junctions. It was so successful that it was soon adopted in other towns, as here in Bedford.

Right: A pleasant, quiet, summer day in the High Street. The war is long over and Britain is growing more prosperous. Lots to look at in Arthur Day's shop window. This was a time when money was easier and housewives wanted the labour- saving devices now available to them. They wanted an electric iron, a washer, a food mixer, a toaster and a vacuum cleaner. They became necessities rather than luxuries. And, since the coronation had been broadcast in 1953, when they had crowded into the homes of those lucky enough to own one, they wanted one too. Never mind the fact that you had to wait for the valves to warm up before anything happened, or that you had to learn how to control the horizontal and vertical holds to prevent the picture from rolling, you had to have one! There were many second hand televisions available after 1955. With the introduction of a second channel called 'Independent Television', those who could afford to do so, sold their old sets and bought a new one that could receive both channels. Now the adverts told you what you should buy, and how to make your teeth whiter for that perfect smile. 'You'll wonder where the yellow went when you clean your teeth..', anyone who lived at the time will fill in the ending. Persil and Omo competed for your attention. Some washing powders contained little specks of blue to bring out the whiteness. Granny used to do that with dolly-blue!

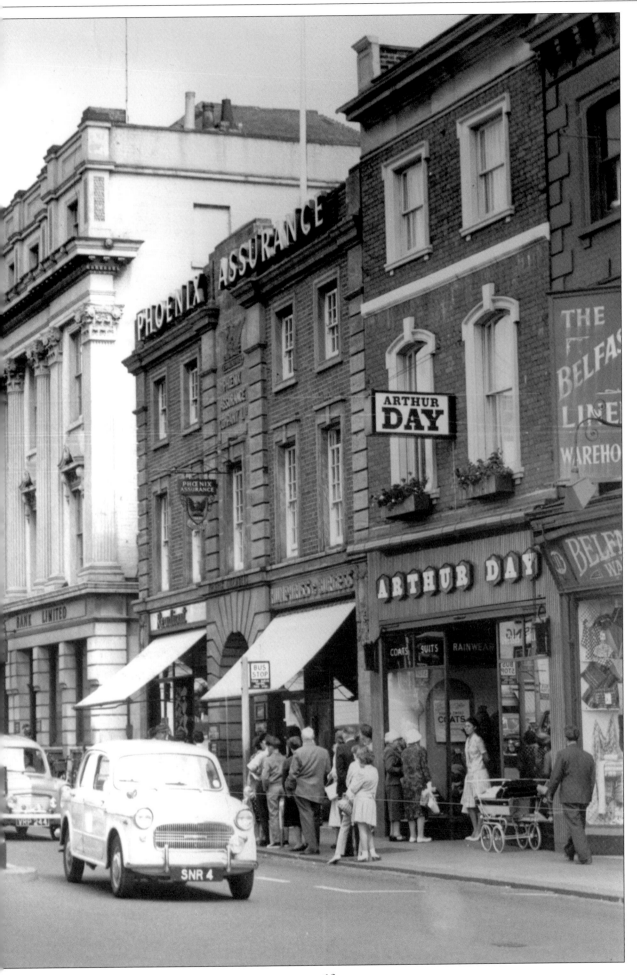

Above: The sun is low in the sky on this beautiful winter's morning, but strong enough to require shade from the blinds above the windows of the shops. The buildings in St Paul's Square have changed little over the years. The Corn Exchange opened for the first time on Sunday 8 January 1940, as the 'Forces Club and Canteen'. The artistes performing at the first show were, Miss Helen Hill (soprano), The Queen's Works Musical Society, the Polychordia Choir, Hans Mahler (violinist), and Miss Daphne Braggins. Their names may not strike a chord in the minds of many, but, during the war years, one band struck a note that would echo in the minds of millions of people over the years. They were the fabulous band of Glenn Miller. He put everyone 'In the Mood' for dancing. The 'Chattanooga Choo Choo' was asked 'won't you carry me home'. The record sold over a million earning the band a Golden Disc Award. 'String of Pearls', and many other memorable tunes, were broadcast from this spot in late 1944. Sadly Glenn Miller was reported missing whilst travelling in an aeroplane to Paris in December 1944. A bust, to commemorate his connection with Bedford, was placed in a niche on the wall of the Corn Exchange 50 years after his death.

This well-known junction of Harpur Street, Silver Street and Midland Road seen here around 1960 is now pedestrianised. Cyclists still ply their way around the town, as much now as they did then. Today there may be lanes planned for them to assist their progress through the traffic. Then they had to risk themselves in the midst of cars, whose brakes were not as keen or reliable as the disc brakes of today. They could buy all the spares they wanted, down the road at Halfords. Baskets were on sale to attach to the handlebars to hold shopping, like the ones these ladies have fixed to their bikes. You could buy locks and chains, but there was less need for them then.

In the 1950s there was a renewed optimism, as the decade began in 1951 with Britain's biggest shop window - the Festival of Britain. Rationing was at an end and there were many new products in the shops. The shops themselves were changing in character, a new idea of 'self-service' was looked upon with suspicion. It was the beginning of a major change in attitudes. Marks and Spencer, scaffolded on this day, may be having a difficult time with its image lately, but then it offered that sense of quality and individual attention to each customer which they enjoyed. Having come through the austerities of the war, it was time to be cosseted and cared for. The 'personal touch' was precisely what they thought they wanted.

Bedford, like many places, grew around a crossing on the river, as the name suggests. This aerial photograph was taken on a clear day in 1952, in the same year as London was experiencing the worst 'smog' it had ever known. Real 'pea-soupers' descended caused by water condensing on particles of soot from the smoke of many coal fires. The smog brought London to a virtual standstill, and many thousands of deaths, from respiratory problems, were attributed to it. In Bedford on this day it is clear enough to see St Paul's spire, pointing like a finger at the Town Bridge. Following the river to the edge of the picture, the

Suspension Bridge can just be seen gracefully spanning the River Great Ouse. The High Street, at right angles to the river, moves up to meet John Bunyan waiting at the crossroads. The Almshouses in Dame Alice Street show clearly. At the top of the picture can be seen the Girls' School in Cardington Road, named after Dame Alice Harpur in 1946. St Mary's Church is still visible beyond Town Bridge, as the Moat House Hotel has not yet been built. It is fascinating to see from such a view the changes which have occurred in a relatively short space of time, and, conversely, how many things have not changed, but have been sensitively preserved.

Above: At five minutes to three on a chilly afternoon in the 1950s, mother and child attempt to cross the High Street in St Paul's Square. Looking both ways and listening for the cars, the 'road drill' is sensibly delivered. Only a few cars are in evidence on this day, which could be a result of petrol rationing brought about by the Suez Crisis. Colonel Nasser had nationalised the canal, through which most of Europe's oil supplies passed. It brought rationing of petrol back to Britain for the second time, on 17 December 1956. Cars are still parked freely with no sign of double yellow lines.

Across at Wells and Company the new 'Utility' furniture is on display - experiments in the use of metal framed chairs, curved arms on simply shaped settees. 'Modern' design had arrived. The radiogram, combining a stereo record player with the radio was on sale. A young performer, who gyrated his hips in a manner considered shocking by adults, but which inspired hysterical admiration from young girls, gained the nickname 'the Pelvis'. Elvis Presley's records sold millions of copies. 'Blue Suede Shoes', 'Teddy Bear', 'Heartbreak Hotel', and many more, have influenced popular music up to the present day.

Facing page: The view has changed very little as we look down the High Street towards Town Bridge, with the exception that St Mary's Church, which is now hidden by the Moat House Hotel, can be seen across the river. Traffic moves in two directions on this day in the fifties. Parked alongside the kerb is a Morris Minor. Designed by Alex Issigonis, who would later design the Mini, it was the first British post-war car to surpass its rivals from the continent. It was an eight horsepower car, which was described as 'compact yet roomy' when it came onto the market.

How many of us remember the police 'case files' in black and white cinema days? In every story a Wolseley police-car, like the one at the bottom of the picture, chased through the streets ringing its bell as it pursued the criminals. Police cars, ambulances and fire engines, in those days, had bells not sirens. Baddies were always about to make their getaway by aeroplane from some disused airfield. At the end of the film Edgar Lustgarten would sum up the reasons why crime did not pay. Films in those days always ended on a happy note and the 'goodies' always won. It was comforting in Westerns to be able to recognise a 'baddy' because he always wore black, and had not shaved, and rode a black horse. A hero, like Roy Rogers, was always immaculate in his white outfit, even at the end of a fierce fight.

High days & holidays

Above: The Chequers Inn, standing on the corner of High Street and Silver Street, is advertising an historic change of purpose in 1911. It is to be opened as a 'Cinematograph Picture Palace', that wonder of the age. A picture of another kind was occupying the news in the August of this year. The world's most famous painting the Mona Lisa by Leonardo da Vinci, had been stolen from the Louvre Museum during the night. Because the picture was so famous, experts believed that it was impossible to sell the picture anywhere in the world. In October of the same year a tavern, on the corner of Sunset and Gower Streets in a little town called

Hollywood, California, had been opened as the first film studio. Because of its all year round sunshine, which provided good lighting for filmmaking, there was speculation that others might well set up studios in the town. Hollywood's connections with the film industry have lasted a little longer than the Palace Theatre in Bedford did, although the name has lived on. The 'Palace' Chambers were built on this spot in 1936. Next door to the Chequers in Silver Street was the town gaol, where Bunyan was imprisoned. There is only a plaque to remind us of this spot where the ideas came to him for what ranks amongst the most famous and best works of English literature.

The Palace Cinema in the High Street, opened in the premises of the former Chequers Inn in 1912, closed its doors to the public in 1936. The Marx brothers were entertaining the world causing mayhem in 'A Night at the Opera'. Groucho, Chico and Harpo literally brought down the curtain on a performance of 'Il Travatore'. The previous year, Shirley Temple won an Oscar for 'her outstanding contribution to screen entertainment during 1934'. Who can forget her cute rendition of the song, 'On the Good Ship Lollipop'? How we all remember going into the side door to the 'four-penny' seats. Unless we succeeded in creeping back into the more expensive seats when the usherette wasn't looking, we had stiff necks at the end of an evening, through looking up at the screen high above. It was a special occasion to accompany our parents into the balcony or the rear stalls. When cinemas first opened the proprietors had some difficulty in persuading the audience that the best seats were at the back, and not the front as at the theatre. At first they thought they were being cheated. There is an advertisement on the wall for 'His Master's Voice- every record available at Fraser's'. We all remember the little dog with its head tilted curiously listening to his master's voice coming through the horn of the gramophone. The first record ever made by that company was a single-sided disc of the Italian tenor, Enrico Caruso, singing an aria from 'Il Pagliacci'.

Above: Topping the bill at the Granada in February 1963 is Helen Shapiro, the young lady with the mature and unique voice. She was 'Walking Back to Happiness' at the height of her career. None in the future would top the bill above the Beatles. Rock-and-roll music was of the fifties, now the sixties would see and hear the Beatles and the Rolling Stones. Elvis had been the 'King' in the previous decade, but now came a new 'Royal Family' from Liverpool. They had been influenced by such singers as Bob Dylan, who had written music with a political message about racism and the nuclear arms race, but soon their style was to set the pattern for all who followed. A new word entered the language in 1963, 'Beatlemania'. Their record, 'She loves you', stood at number one spot for four weeks and sold over a million copies.

What a show these fans are about to see. Dave Allen, who was to host his own long running television show, poked gentle fun at everyone whilst sitting on his bar stool with a glass in his hand. Who can forget the response from the church when he performed funny sketches targeting them? Kenny Lynch went on to be equally successful.

Above right: It is difficult to believe that this bridge was built as early as 1888. Its sweeping, functional lines, and delicate lattice girder construction makes it seem as though it was built only yesterday. The Marquess of Tavistock was kept very busy in 1888. He was guest of honour at the opening of the park, and he was also invited to open thie

Suspension Bridge on the same day, 11 July. This well-known landmark was designed by John J Webster, and was renovated in 1983-84. It achieved the status of 'a listed building' in 1995. Its graceful span makes a good marker for the members of the rowing club as they glide beneath it, and forms an interesting background for the many visitors when they take their photographs of the swans and the river. Having mounted the steps, the man in the picture will soon reach the less steep asphalt surface where he can pause and look up to his right at the magnificent view of the river. With parks on either side, his view will be clear up to the Town Bridge. At the time that it was built it cost the princely sum of five hundred pounds. For the pleasure it gives and the status it has acquired with time, it was money well spent.

More Memories of **BEDFORD**

ven the fairy has decided to descend from the tree to hear the story at the Howard Home. 'Are you sitting comfortably? Then I'll begin. Once upon a time..' And they are sitting nicely on best behaviour for the moment. The floor will get a little harder for the boy who has had to sit there. Has he misbehaved, or is it only because it suits the composition of this picture? It would make an excellent, although rather sentimental, Victorian Christmas card. Maybe the story for tonight is that new one which has been written by a Scottish writer James Barrie as a London stage-play. 'Peter Pan or the Boy Who Wouldn't Grow Up', opened at the Duke

of York's Theatre on 27 December 1904. Appropriately the story had been written for five boys, like the ones in this picture. Barrie was their guardian. Peter Pan received a strong challenge from Christopher Robin and his friend Winnie the Pooh, when they appeared on the scene in 1926. Written by A. A. Milne, there are no frightening characters like Captain Hook, or crocodiles that bite off hands. It was a time when parents were beginning to question the kind of reading material that their children were being subjected to, and parents and teachers thought that some corrupted the children. But the comics are still here and as popular as ever.

The Bedfordshire Times recorded this occasion, when, on 5 January 1940 the Ouse froze over and people were skating on the ice. The last time it had done so, they said, was in the winter of 1891. In 1891 the paper told of Mr Herbert Percy Saunderson, founder of Elstow Engineering Works, who brought a horse-drawn sledge along and gave joy rides on the ice. What a sight it must have been. He called the sledge, which he had built himself, the 'American Dodger'.

On this day in 1940, almost as if the enemy would not attack when the weather was cold, the war is forgotten. All thoughts were on the task of staying upright on the slippery surface. Three days later, on 8 January, butter, sugar, and bacon were rationed. But there were still many good things left: one was to sit in front of the warm coal fire, after the fun on the ice. Assuming it hadn't gone out while you were sliding. It wasn't safe to bank it too high, and it was essential to put the fireguard around. So often sparks would singe the canvas-backed rug. Many will have helped to make such a rug by cutting strips of material and pulling them through the weft of the canvas with a hook to make tufts. Trimming them level with a pair of scissors made an acceptable finish to the design.

Right: It was a wet day in July 1888 when the park was first opened, the same year as the pneumatic bicycle tyre was invented, for which these two loving cyclists are no doubt grateful. In 1888 Jack the Ripper stalked East End streets on foggy nights. It was also the year in which the first Kodak camera was made, and what better scene than this to put it to use? The tennis courts to the south of the bandstand were not in the original designs for the park. This area was intended for archery ranges. This fine example of a Victorian bandstand, although small in scale, has often been used as the model for others. It stands at the opposite end of the path from the pavilion as a complementary element in the park's plan. The Mayor was ill, and the Deputy Mayor, Alderman Jabez Carter, officiated in his place. The weather was not good, and a crowd had gathered at the gate ready for the official unlocking with a golden key. The Marquess of Tavistock was to perform that important duty, but his train was delayed an hour. The Deputy Mayor, the children from Harpur Elementary School, the Bedfordshire Volunteers, the Engineer Corps waited in the drizzling rain for his arrival. It was reported that he performed his duty well and duly opened the gate, using the golden key. The weather improved slightly and the Deputy Mayor conducted a guided tour around the park to the sound of the brass band.

Below: Skating on what we hope is not thin ice. Mum gives the necessary support to the daughter, as the dog pulls dad along. He and the boy on the sledge seem to have the right idea, allowing others to pull them. Unlike the moulded plastic sledges of today, sledges were often home made, probably by granddad. They had iron runners. All kinds of myths grew as to the best way in which to improve the sledge's performance. Rub them with lard and they would skim the surface, or was it oil, or Vaseline or something we have now forgotten? Funny how, when we were their age, the cold was not felt. It was not until you returned to the warmth of the house that fingers and toes tingled as the circulation returned to normal. The boys seem to be competent skaters. Perhaps they developed their skills at the Glider Rink on roller skates. In Bedford, as in many parts of the country, roller-skating became popular. Introduced in America in 1910, it achieved respectability, as figure dancing on roller skates became a recognised sport. These children will not be familiar with Sonja Henie, who won her first gold medal at the Olympics at the tender age of fourteen. She then went on to win two more and ten successive world titles, before turning professional in 1936. She starred in many films and inspired lots of young skaters.

Memorable moments

There has been a school in Bedford for hundreds of years, even before Edward VI granted Bedford licence to establish a 'free and perpetual Grammar School'in 1552. On early plans of Bedford clues can be found as to where the first school, run by monks, was built. Mill Street is shown to have been called Mill Lane, and even earlier to have had the name 'Scholestreet'. The Reverend Edmund Greene ran a school perhaps as early as 1548. Then along came that benefactor Sir William Harpur who provided the school with premises in St Paul's Square, with an adjoining house for Edmund Greene. Harpur's 1566 endowment was one of the most significant influences on the town throughout the nineteenth and much of the twentieth centuries. Many young people have had much to thank him for over the years. Here we see the girls from the Girls Modern School in 1932, six years before their school moved to Cardington Road. It was renamed the Dame Alice Harpur School in 1946. 'La crème de la crème', walk by as the traffic is stopped by the policeman. All smart in their uniform. What lessons on discipline and self-control can be learnt from these girls and their teachers?

Almost surreal, like a scene from a modern space film, the massive shape floats menacingly above De Parys Avenue in August 1918. A giant dirigible (which means 'able to be steered or directed') moves gracefully across the sky. It was the R31 constructed in a huge shed at Cardington, near Bedford. A much bigger airship, the R101 was 777 feet in length, two feet longer than Germany's Graff Zeppelin. It proved to be too heavy, and there were many problems during construction. Drastic steps were taken to rectify them. Leaving on its maiden flight to Karachi, it arrived over Beauvais, northwest of Paris, and was seen to be flying very low. Its nose dipped as it fought into a strong wind and it crashed and burst into flames on 5 October 1930. Only six men of the fifty-six on board survived. 'Zeppelins',named after the German Count responsible for their early development, were used during the First World War to drop bombs on London for the first time. The airship ultimately failed as a weapon of war, but in peacetime it was seen as the future of travel. In 1929 the Graf Zeppelin made, what was described as, 'a circumnavigation of the world', covering 20,500 miles. It was in the air for a total of twelve days. It flew over Wembley Stadium in 1930, making a friendly pass over a national championship football match attended by 92,000 people, including King George V.

Below: Straight backed and marching with precision, the Women's Land Army look spick and span in their brown and green uniforms, as they turn eyes left to receive the salute from His Majesty the King and his much loved Queen. When a bomb hit Buckingham Palace, the King is reputed to have said that he felt better, because he could now identify with the people who had had their houses bombed. He had refused to leave the country, as some had suggested he should, because he regarded it to be his duty to stand by the people. The people had great regard for him because of it. He had accepted the crown when his brother abdicated and wore it gracefully. When the end of the war was announced on VE day, he gave one of his first radio broadcasts to the nation. Everyone held their breath, as they all knew that he had been afflicted with a terrible stammer all his life. He delivered his speech without the slightest hint of difficulty and many knew what an effort it was to him and applauded that as much as the words he spoke. 'The dreadful shadow has passed', he said, 'Let us remember those who will not come back - they are not with us at the moment of rejoicing'.

Right: There is hardly a head in the crowd without some form of hat. The teachers are wearing their mortarboards, seldom seen now except in the comics. The shape of the homburg hat, and the soft felt head hugging 'flapper' hat, is a demonstration of how the technology of a time can influence the fashion. The respectful crowd watch as the scouts proudly lead the school children past St Peter's Green. The Scout movement, as a separate organisation, was not the original intention of Sir Robert Baden-Powell when he wrote his book, *Scouting for Boys*. The book was intended for use by existing youth organisations, but his clear ideas about the development of character and independence stirred the imaginations of generations of boys, and the scouting movement began as an organisation in its own right. Soon guiding for girls followed the pattern. Through teaching them the skills of camping, orienteering, signalling, and first aid amongst others, their self-confidence was built. The ability to tie a reliable knot, or cook over a campfire, surprisingly, have their links with tasks needing to be done in adult life. Those who were scouts or guides know how these experiences have influenced, and shaped, their lives. Sir Robert Baden-Powell could not have dreamed that the movement would become so popular and soon spread to other countries throughout the world.

At the start of the war men who were in 'reserved occupations' could join the armed forces if they so wished, but soon the Government had to place some jobs under the 'Essential Work Order'. This meant that workers could not be sacked, neither could they leave if they wanted to. Farming fell under this category, but it was only the farmer himself who was classed as being in a 'reserved occupation' and not his farm workers. So it was that the Women's Land Army was born. The women went into the jobs made vacant as the men moved to the factories or into the armed forces. Large numbers of women

were drafted into war work. Unmarried women between the ages of 20 and 30 were the first to be called upon, but by 1943 all women, not looking after children under the age of 14, were conscripted into war work. The government had a shock when so many women volunteered that they had to set up nurseries to look after the children. The women were drafted into jobs which had traditionally been considered the domain of men. They operated machines to make munitions, they joined the Civil Defence, they joined the Women's Voluntary Service and they ploughed fields. They tackled any job needing to be done.

obbin came to the rescue in March 1947 just as his father had when the river flooded in 1918. The exceptionally heavy snows had thawed rapidly and the river burst its banks in several places. Here, in Cardington Road, the only one with wet feet is the horse. It looks a little precarious for the boys balanced on the back, but what fun! A horse and cart were still a fairly common sight after the war. They did not need the scarce petrol. The milkman and his horse-drawn cart were slowly being replaced by a flat backed lorry or van, but a few still worked, some of whom provided the milk from a churn measured into your jug. Stories were often told of the milkman's horse that decided to go home one cold day. When the milkman returned from making a delivery to a house, the horse had gone. It was later found back in its warm stable. A flat backed cart, such as this one would be there to lend a hand for furniture removals and light haulage. Sacks of coal arrived on such transport and were tipped into the coal shed prior to 1956 when the Clean Air Act was passed.

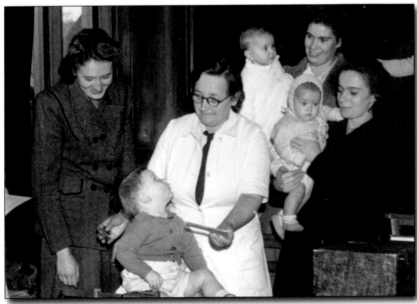

flour, little realising that this treatment would continue into school years with regular examination of teeth, and, worst of all, close inspections of the hair for any signs of head-lice. 'Nits!' oh the shame of it!

Top: The lettering says, 'Hush a Bye Baby', but there will be no sleep or quiet whilst these two Americans from the 306 Bombardment Group based at Thurleigh, North of Bedford, visit the Victoria Ward of the hospital. The one leaning over Matron's shoulder, is called Jimmy Czinder. He and his friend have brought gifts for the unfortunate girl in the tubular metal cot. 'Got any gum, chum?' was the cry to any American soldiers or airmen from the children whose sweets were on ration. The generous servicemen often distributed chewing gum or chocolate if they could. They were great ambassadors for their country and many long-lasting friendships were made during this time. The generosity of the American people continued after the war with CARE parcels containing anything that could be of use to the people of Britain and Europe. In 1947 the US Secretary of State, George Marshall, offered financial help to Europe. He said that the hardships suffered by Europe were a new threat to world peace. All the Soviet-dominated countries rejected the offer, others, Britain included, accepted the generous help. British Foreign Secretary Ernest Bevin, said a 'thank you', for Europe was experiencing hardships as great as those suffered during the war. We may have had little in the way of resources, but we did have some pretty nurses!

Above: As a reaction, no doubt, to the lack of food and supplies during the war years, doctors and mothers were concerned about the health of children. Many of us can still remember the days when we had milk at school. Most of us did not really mind this method of making sure that we received our measured amount of calcium, but the line should have been drawn when someone decided that cod-liver oil was good for us! Those who were subjected to the regular spoonful will probably shudder at the very thought of it. Close behind it came the orange juice. One was never sure whether this was to prevent rickets, or some other such problem, or merely a ploy to get us to take the cod-liver oil. Records were kept of our weight and height. Children were immunised against diseases that had been fatal in the past.
The child looks questioningly at the stranger and wonders why he or she is being treated like a bag of

Above: Proud mothers hold their healthy babies high at this show at the Town Hall in 1946. These mothers may well have been concerned that their daughters might grow up in a world which had just been introduced to a new skimpy garment called a bikini. The name was taken, by their inventor, Louis Reard, from the islands in the South Pacific where the Americans had tested nuclear weapons. This two-piece swimsuit concealed very little of the woman's body and caused a minor explosion of a different kind in 1946. The Labour Government had come into power the previous year, with a promise to provide a better life for the whole nation, poor and rich alike. They were concerned about the health and welfare of the nation and working towards the introduction of the National Health Service. These babies and their mothers and fathers could now receive free treatment 'from cradle to grave'. The Health Minister, Aneurin Bevan, faced some opposition to the plans from dentists and members of the British Medical Association. The Prime minister, Clement Attlee expected some difficulties, but he assured the nation that they could be overcome.

Not only babies were being judged in 1946, but also Nazi leaders for their war crimes. Hess and Goering, Hitler's former deputies, were amongst those who appeared at court in Nuremburg. Twelve of the twenty-two being tried received the death sentence for their crimes against humanity.

Above right: It was a Sunday in March 1943 when many housewives woke up to discover that they had a different milkman bringing their daily 'pinta'. The government had imposed zoning. Milkmen could only deliver within their allocated areas. The idea was that it would make better

use of materials and resources. No one can be sure whether the plan was any more efficient, but it was another demonstration of the powers, and the speed with which those powers could be implemented. So Ernie, 'who drove the fastest milk cart in the west' according to Benny Hill, had to drive it where he was told to go. The women of the Land Army worked hard to ensure that milk production was efficient. They were in the front line of the 'Dig for Victory' drive inspired by the government, ploughing every acre of land they could use and thus increasing food production. Extra land in Bedford was turned over to the production of food. Children were given their milk in school to ensure that they received the benefit. Many of us will remember that we were glad that we liked it, and made sure that we sat next to the boy in our class who didn't. The youngest in school were also given orange juice. Very few refused that, and there were some funny noises coming from straws as they sucked the very last drops from the bottom of the bottle.

Right: The nineteen-year-old Princess Elizabethhas all the confidence, maturity, and bearing acquired through years of preparation for her life as the future queen. She shows her natural ability to put people at their ease in her presence. She leans forward a little, and looks attentively at the old soldier, and he knows that these small signs are indicative of her interest in what he has to say. All who were presented to her on this day in February 1946, commented on how well aware she was of all they had done during the recent struggle. Standing proudly erect, the old soldiers display their service medals. One will brave the cold damp day, and hold his raincoat over his arm, so that the brightly coloured ribbons, and medals polished as brightly as his shoes, can be seen. Most men not in uniform wear a fashionable homburg or a bowler hat. Headwear, more than anything else has always been a way of expressing personality. Throughout history, hats have also often been a statement of class or rank. Although each stop she made was brief, the Princess left a lasting impression on many. She delivered some well-deserved thanks to the people of Bedford for their work over the last few difficult years. She warned that there were still hard times ahead. Food and resources were scarce throughout Europe, and it would be many years before they would begin to feel the benefits of their labours.

Below: Bayonets fixed and willing to do their duty again if required, they stand smartly to attention as they receive a close inspection from the young Princess Elizabeth. Her blue woollen costume, with hat and veil to match, complemented by a simple row of pearls and a brooch, helped brighten a dull and wet day. The wait may have been a long one for these chaps, but well worth it for the experience which they could pass on to their families in years to come. They knew that they were the lucky ones who had survived the previous years. Now that the victory celebrations were over came the hard work of cleaning up and building. The Princess told them that they would be still needed in the next few years. They may not have known that the Princess and her sister, Princess Margaret had slipped out of Buckingham Palace, accompanied by two army officers, to join the crowds singing and dancing in the Mall on VE Day. Amongst that crowd was a young jazz musician with his trombone playing 'Roll out the Barrel', 'Hi, Hi, Hippee Hippee Hi', and many other tunes for the crowd to sing along with. They had lifted him high not knowing then that Humphrey Lyttelton would be famous for his music in the coming years. We will probably never know if the two Princesses danced and sang 'Knees up Mother Brown', along with the rest.

Below centre: On Thursday 14 February 1946 the nineteen-year-old Princess Elizabeth visited Bedford to open the Exhibition of Agricultural Work and Handicrafts staged by the Women's Land Army, and held in the Corn Exchange. She had arrived in Bedford at 11.30 a.m. and was met by the Lord Lieutenant and taken for lunch at The Swan Hotel. The exhibition was open for three days and demonstrated 'How victory was won on the food front'. The local newspapers reported how the thatched roofs above some of the stalls created the right atmosphere. The extent of their contribution to victory was evident, the local paper said. The displays received a touch of colour from fairy lights and above the platform was a replica of the Bedfordshire and Hertfordshire Regimental badge, decorated with greenery. These girls had come from all walks of life and had had to learn the skills of ploughing, sowing and getting maximum efficiency from the land. They had built and maintained cowsheds and sheep pens and proudly tackled jobs which they would never have imagined doing before the war began. They had dug ditches and laid land drains. All the achievements were displayed in front of an admiring and grateful public.

Bottom: No disparaging remarks about 'women drivers', but only admiration for the women in the brown and green uniforms, as they drive past the podium where the Princess was taking the salute. Only a little further and it will be a smart 'eyes right'. Lining the road is a crowd who have come into town for this expression of thanks to these hard working women who, in the words of Princess Elizabeth, were still needed. 'The country still needs you. The immediate peril is over, but no one can fail to realise what lies ahead is not peace with plenty, but peace with grievous scarcity'. She went on to tell them that the work in the future will be of equal importance to that done over the six years of war. Her message was so very true. Farms and livestock had been lost and there was a food shortage throughout Europe. Everything was still horded and waste was 'sinful'. Mum and Grandmother encouraged children to eat everything on their plate. 'Don't help the squander bug'. They grew with a healthy attitude and a sense of appreciation for whatever they were given. 'We can't afford waste', was still the cry. Scarcity was the enemy now. In America there was a time of plenty. They sent CARE parcels (Co-operative for American Remittances to Europe). Over twelve million tonnes of grain alone was shipped from America to Europe in 1946.

ploughs, and manure distributors (muck spreaders as the girls would call them), drove by. The parade of equipment gave the crowd a good idea of the farming methods employed and of the splendid work these women had done. The bands of the Sea Cadet Corps and the Army Cadet Force marched in the procession.

Left: Is it a car or is it a bike? It is steered with handlebars, but rides on four wheels. According to records the first motorcycles were seen around 1902. However it is described, these two young men, entered in a rally c1950, can be justifiably proud of the condition of this early machine. Dated 1900 it has, however, conformed to the requirements of the 1903 Motor Car Act, when registration numbers were introduced, and a driving licence was required. What price would such a personalised plate command today? The passenger sits comfortably enough with his feet tucked in behind the curved dash panel, even if rather exposed. The pedal assisted petrol motor drives the axle to the rear wheels and away you go. We laugh now at the idea that a man with a flag had to herald the approach of vehicle in 1895. The Highways Act was sensible for a time when horseless vehicles on the roads were extremely heavy, on the whole steam powered, and very noisy. The man waving the flag gave riders and drivers time to calm their horses before they steamed past at a speed of 2 mph in the towns, and a breath taking 4 mph in the country. By the time this 'car' was on the roads, the 1896 'Emancipation Act' was passed, lifting the need for the flag and increasing the top speed limit to 12 mph.

Top: Six hundred members of the Women's' Land Army marched past the podium on that day in February 1946. Shops and schools closed early and young and old alike lined the streets to cheer Her Royal Highness, Princess Elizabeth. Despite the gloomy wet weather she had toured around the town in the morning and was cheered all the way by the large crowd of people who had come into Bedford for the occasion. She paused on her journey to stop at the Town Hall, where she received the loyal address of welcome from the Mayor, Aldermen and Burgesses of the Borough. She took the salute in High Street. The band of the Royal Air Force heralded the approach of the Land Army volunteers. The girls were impressive in their familiar brown and green uniforms, and they marched as proudly erect as any guardsman. Behind them came a sample of the vehicles they used. As important to the war effort as any tank, the tractors,

Harrison & Rowley - a moving story

HARRISON & ROWLEY
34 36 FOSTER HILL ROAD
BEDFORD
ARE CONTINUING THEIR
GREAT FURNISHING
TELEPHONE 2697

SALE

DINING SUITES, BEDROOM SUITES, AND
THREE-PIECE SUITES at Greatly Reduced Prices
Large Stocks of
CARPETS, LINOLEUMS, & RUGS
to be cleared
A SPLENDID OPPORTUNITY TO RE-FURNISH AT LOW
COST   CALL AND INSPECT

'H&R the Best by Far' takes some beating as a memorable slogan. Today the name of Harrison & Rowley is recognised not only for running the town of Bedford's premier furniture store but also for its world class removals and storage business. The company's fine reputation has been growing constantly ever since the firm was established in 1922.

This family owned business is one of Bedford's flagship retailers. As it moves into the 21st century it is now confidently writing the next chapter in its success story, a chapter which takes the company into the new millennium still firmly sticking to the aim of retaining the traditional values of old fashioned quality and service whilst enthusiastically embracing modern technology.

Harrison & Rowley has come to its position of prominence on the local retail scene whilst still continuing to trade from its landmark premises in Foster Hill Road where it all began eight decades ago.

The firm began life in the 1920s as a small business dealing in the sale of second hand furniture and goods. Who then could have guessed that Harrison and Rowley would one day become one of the area's most prestigious businesses?

Today the firm specialises in offering a vast range of quality furniture, displayed over two floors of its attractive showrooms, representing leading manufacturers such as Ercol, Parker Knoll, Peter Guild and G Plan. As complete house furnishers Harrison and Rowley offer a huge choice of plain, patterned and tonal floor coverings available to suit every room in the house, and to suit all tastes. The company supplies a complete fitting service by fully trained fitters. Other services include the cleaning of carpets and upholstery, as well as the refitting and adaption of carpets. Furthermore, within the showroom is a curtain gallery, offering a vast array of

Above: *An advertisement from January 1936.*
Below: *The firm's premises during the 1953 coronation.*

curtains and blinds, with a full made-to-measure fitting service.

To complement the firm's unrivalled reputation for quality goods Harrison & Rowley proudly boasts a professional team of staff which offers a wealth of experience and expertise. At the helm is Jeff Winrow who joined the company more than 40 years ago and worked his way up to become managing director in 1969. Prominent members of staff include David Curtis, Store Manager, who has notched up a quarter of a century with Harrison & Rowley and has been in the furniture trade for more than 30 years; Brian Barratt, Salesperson, has even longer experience in the trade. John Lilly, Carpet Manager, also has many years of expertise as well as Alex Timms, Sales person, another important member of the team who has a number of years behind him. Stewart Harrison, Administrator, joined the firm in the late 1990s after moving to the UK from South Africa.

Also housed in Foster Hill Road is the accounts department, made up of Glynis Winrow (Jeff's wife) and the Accounts Manager, Frances Smart.

Karl Winrow, Jeff's son, is the most recent family member to work for the firm and is now IT Manager. In the late 1990s he started work with the firm as a trainee manager like his father before him.

Karl is responsible for updating and maintaining the complex wide area computer network that he set up, which links the firm's three sites together, increasing the efficiency of the work force, vehicles and most importantly communication. Karl has set about taking the firm into the new millennium, using the latest equipment and technology, including establishing a company website offering on-line quotes with a view in the future to selling on-line

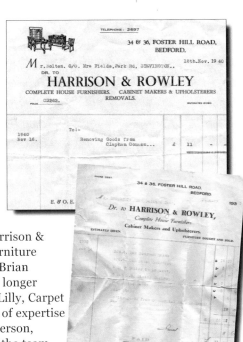

(www.harrisonandrowley.com), without compromising good old-fashioned customer service.

With outstanding service extending to after-sales care, a large customer car park at the rear of the premises and the guarantee of top quality goods at competitive prices it is no exaggeration to describe Harrison & Rowley as simply the best. And better still is promised for the future. But how did it all begin?

Not surprisingly the firm was founded by a Mr Harrison and a Mr Rowley. The partnership began in 1922. That partnership soon ended with the death of Rowley in 1923 leaving Tom Harrison as sole proprietor to be eventually assisted by his son and successor Tim Harrison.

The new business had begun at 34 Foster Hill Road selling second hand furniture. Transport was needed to deliver the goods sold and at first a horse and cart were used. A van eventually replaced the horse and cart, though when the van was found to be standing idle for much of the time work was found carrying out removals. The business was destined never to move from Foster Hill Road though various changes were made over the years as adjacent property was acquired including numbers 22b, 34 and 36. A nearby building was acquired where renovations to

Above: Invoices which show two of the company's letterheads. ***Below:*** *Retail staff today.*

second hand furniture and prams were made, at one time employing three full-time upholsterers and one French polisher.

By the outbreak of the second world war the firm, now describing itself on its letterheads as 'Harrison & Rowley Complete House Furnishers Cabinet Makers and Upholsterers and Removals', was the proud owner of two vans purchased second hand. That pride didn't last long: the two vans were soon commandeered for war service. When the firm eventually bought another, larger van its primary use was to bring people from London to Bedford during the Blitz.

Jeff Winrow joined the firm at the age of 16 after working part time for Harrison & Rowley whilst still a school boy. His mother and father ran the Wellington public house which overlooked the back of the Harrison & Rowley shop so it was the obvious place for

him to earn a little extra money during the holidays. Jeff would later recall those early days. In those days the shop closed at lunch-time and if a delivery van arrived when no staff were about young Jeff would nip

Above: A 1931 picture of the work force. From left to right: Tim Harrison, a removal man, Zena Robertson, Harry Fensom, Reg Rowney.
Top: Bedford Town Bridge in 1951 with one of the company's vans in the bottom centre.

across the road and help unload. Jeff was, in his own words, 'only a secondary-modern schoolboy' but he liked to think he was blessed with plenty of common sense; Tim Harrison was so impressed with Jeff's keenness that he offered him a full time job when he left school. He certainly always had the knack of getting on with people and so was given a job in sales.

At the time Tim Harrison was already planning for his eventual retirement and when it became obvious that neither of his sons was particularly keen to follow their father in the business he made Jeff a trainee manager, grooming him for eventual succession.

Tim Harrison eventually sold his interest in the business and emigrated with his family to South Africa in 1970. That was not however the end of the Harrison family's involvement with the firm: in 1999 Tim Harrison's nephew Stewart Harrison moved back to the UK and now works for the company.

Back in the 1960s however the owner's idea of training was to show young Jeff Winrow something then let him get on with it. Jeff was put in the workshop, sent off on removals, did carpet and floor laying and French-polishing. He may not have become an expert at all these things, but at least he could do them all. When Jeff had been with the firm ten years Tim Harrison decided to retire to South Africa and he gave Jeff the opportunity to buy the business. But of course to buy a business one needed money, rather a lot. Jeff, then just 25 years old, trawled the banks and finance houses but could find no-one to back him.

Eventually however Jeff was put in touch with Albert Arthur Jones the local MP who had twice been the Mayor of Bedford and was well known as an acute businessman; he was the making of Jeff Winrow who today graciously acknowledges the enormous debt he would owe him, had it not been for Mr Jones the present firm would simply not exist. Jones took an inspired business risk on the young Jeff,

Left and below: *Two of the early vans owned by the firm.*

entering into a 50:50 partnership with him. Jones put up the finance and left Jeff to run the business. Surprisingly Mr Jones never once tried to interfere. It proved to be a wise decision and an even wiser investment. The Winrow/Jones partnership was set up in April 1968 and in the first year the turnover was £50,000. Today it is approaching £5 million.

In 1970 the firm closed its second hand furniture department to concentrate purely on a wider selection of new furniture made by top manufacturers such as Schreiber. The ending of second hand sales ended an era for the firm. Increasing sales enabled increased investment, in 1975 for example £30,000 was spent on increasing the size of the shop from 3,000 to 11,500 sq.ft whilst the inside was completely refurbished.

Today the retail side of the Harrison & Rowley business is part of AIS, the largest independent furniture buying group in the country, supplying the country's leading 500 independent retailers which gives the pricing edge over the multiple stores.

A third generation of customers now provides a very broad customer base comprising all ages. But then there will always be a ready market for good quality furniture, carpets and curtains sold at a competitive price. Despite the passage of years the firm remains a family run business offering a first class service to customers. Harrison & Rowley is today the only major independent retailer in Bedford town centre, in contrast with the many multiples. The firm has considered moving even closer to the town centre but people know where it is, and of course it has ample car parking space. Where can one park in town these days? Some people inevitably moan about retail parks on the outskirts of town but the fact remains that they are popular with the public. People want to take their cars and be able to park. Harrison & Rowley may not be on a retail park but its location remains far more accessible than if it were in the heart of the town centre. In addition to retailing furnishings, the business also operates a world-wide removals service which now has offices in three counties.

When planning a house move, the quality of service and price are paramount; together with considering the security of the company, its resources and experience. All the staff at Harrison & Rowley are specialists in the latest techniques, materials and technology. Sales representatives quickly assess customers' removal needs and supply detailed

quotes where applicable. All materials and equipment are provided as part of a professional packing service and everything is treated with the utmost care and attention.

Harrison & Rowley vehicles have become a familiar sight at cross-Channel ports as thousands of families successfully relocate to all parts of Europe helped by the company's agents handling all documentation and customs formalities as well as delivery, unpacking and setting up a new home.

Many customers require their effects to be stored. Harrison & Rowley operates a convenient, safe and secure domestic containerised storage facility in a fully equipped, modern purpose-built warehouse. Commercial moves are catered for with skilled crews operating over weekends to minimise the impact on business, archive document service offers businesses the chance to maximise storage space at their own premises.

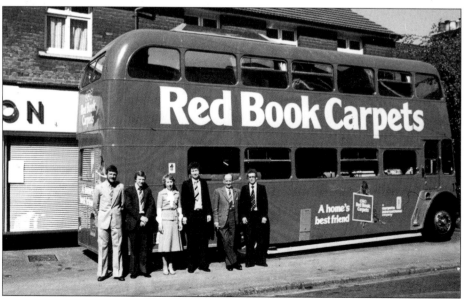

Above left: *A view of the front of the shop, 2001.* ***Left:*** *A group photo of the staff during an autumn promotional event in 1980.*

that need an aircraft hanger, the largest warehouse on the estate at 20,000 sq. ft, was taken in Rope Walk.

By the end of the 1980s a purpose built storage facility was required and Jeff Winrow and John Thomson went seriously looking for land in Bedford, though initially without any luck. At the time Brittains of St Neots decided to sell the removals and storage sector of their business and fortuitously it had an acre of land partly developed for its storage activities. Harrison & Rowley purchased the Brittains

John Thomson joined the firm in 1979 as removal manager; he already had 13 years' experience within the industry but joined H&R after Jeff Winrow offered him a free hand to put in place innovations and systems for the future. John started out based at Foster Hill Road and at the storage depots in Iddesleigh Road and St. Leonard's Street. Over the next 20 years led by John the removal side of the business would grow from just three removal vans using 4,000 sq. ft. of storage space with two office staff to a business which today operates a fleet of over 25 removal pantechnicons, has 40,000 sq. ft. of warehousing and a staff of 60.

Following John Thomson's arrival conventional storage was soon changed to containerised storage. Within a year the popularity of containerised storage had grown to such an extent that far larger premises were urgently needed: in 1981 to meet

removals and storage business; thus enabling the construction of a new state-of-the-art 10,000 sq ft containerised warehouse. As a result of the Brittains acquisition and subsequent building, the removals and storage division of H&R moved to St Neots.

St Neots was the firm's first purpose-built premises. Areas of the new warehouse were developed for the storage of new furniture for the retail division with suite racks and carpet racks as well as storage for the removal of personal household effects.

As part of the ongoing expansion Harrison & Rowley became founder members of Britannia Movers International PLC, a national consortium of removal firms.

Top: *An early removal van.*
Above: *Unloading a storage container.*

Britannia Movers International plc is a consortium of local owned and operated removal companies; each is long established in their own area and all have united together to provide a full range of moving and storage services at home and abroad. Britannia was established in March 1981 and since that date has grown in size from the original five founder members, Harrison & Rowley being one, to over 50 companies within the UK. The group has a combined estimated removals and storage sales turnover of approximately £95 million annually. In September 1999, as part of its development, BMI became a plc.

The concept by which the group operates is simple yet effective and based on 'partnership' principles. This culture of sharing extends throughout all spheres of the organisation, from the introduction of new technological developments, the exchange of new ideas, co-ordinating job and traffic movements, sales and marketing, training, group purchasing and many more. Improved working practices and skills-based training courses, developed by the group training school have helped to create a reputation for quality second-to-none. With over 400 vehicles and 1,200 staff, the group is a UK market leader, carrying out many thousands of moves annually. Britannia also provides global moving and storage services to over 20,000 destinations world-wide by sea and air. Britannia Movers International; a wholly owned and managed British company with the experience to excel for you!

Britannia Harrison & Rowley became the first Bedfordshire removals company to be awarded the prestigious British Standard EN 12522 (Domestic removals for private Individuals). Statistics had shown that moving home could be one of the most stressful experiences anyone is likely to encounter. The new standard had been created to specifically cover furniture removal services provided to private individuals and to ensure that holders of the certificate would minimise the stress of moving for their clients - certification being awarded only to those companies which had demonstrated their ability to meet stringent quality requirements on a day to day basis and price their services accordingly.

Another firm, Pink & Jones Removals of Kettering, came up for sale in 1996 : that new business would become the group's major area of development in the late 1990s. Pink & Jones was another venerable firm with more than a century of history behind it. WA Pink had arrived in Kettering from his native Yorkshire with a donkey and cart in the final decades of the 19th century and set up a small coal and wood delivery business. Pink started moving furniture during the quiet summer months when fuel was not required and soon began to specialise in moving Church of England clergy. He ran the business single-handed until 1933 when GF Jones joined him. In the 1960s and 70s the company

Below: *The warehouse today, with two of the new vans outside.*

specialised in removals to and from Scotland benefiting from the to-ing and fro-ing of Scottish families employed by Stewarts & Lloyds at Corby. GF Jones took over the firm from WA Pink and on his own subsequent retirement sold the firm to B Smith upon whose own retirement would sell it to Harrison & Rowley.

At the time of the Harrison & Rowley take-over Pink & Jones was housed in three separate buildings which made operating complicated and costly. A new 18,500 sq. ft office and warehouse complex would eventually be built on a one acre site to replace the 27,000 sq. ft which had been spread over the three sites. The planning, building and moving to new premises would take two years following which the company then focused its attention on upgrading and refurbishing its fleet of vehicles . Quality new removal lorries attract cost

Top: Old photo of P&J.
Above: The Pink & Jones Warehouse.

in the region of £75,000 whilst refurbishment of existing vehicles will on average cost £10,000. This process is an on-going scenario whereby a mixture of new vehicles and refurbishment is continually being carried out between the three divisions in order to maintain a professional image.

Today the Harrison & Rowley business remains as a complete house furnishers at its Bedford store alongside an ever growing removals and containerised storage, European and Overseas removals. The Britannia Harrison & Rowley group runs dozens of commercial vehicles operating throughout the UK and Europe - and through the Britannia Group is able to ship to 20,000 destinations world-wide.

What's the secret of the firm's long-running climb to the top? According to Jeff Winrow, the answer lies in striving for the highest standards of quality, reliability and integrity with good managerial skills, techniques and training programmes, as well as keeping up to date with innovation, fashion and trends.

In the decades since the firm was founded in 1922 by Messrs Harrison and Rowley there can be few residents of Bedford who have not visited the firm's showrooms or indeed used their removals service. The founders would however undoubtedly have been astonished at the growth which has occurred to their once-tiny second hand furniture store. Having witnessed the entrepreneurism in action which has occurred since 1968 however few of the citizens of Bedford will be astonished at H&R's present prominent position.

The People's War

Above: The soldier in the photograph is demonstrating the use of a Bren gun as an anti-aircraft weapon at a Territorial Army recruiting display in front of the Swan Hotel on 25 April 1939. If the statue outside the Swan Hotel could speak, it would give an account of the conditions faced in the South Africa War against the Boers. Some of the older men in this group could have been involved in that same war which ended in 1902, the year after the death of Queen Victoria, and may well have some graphic stories to tell this 'youngster' about it. When they went to war in 1914 army officers still rode on horseback. They could tell him how they had had to contend with chlorine gas whilst they were in the trenches. In December 1939 a battalion of the County Regiment was reformed and absorbed the Bedfordshire National Defence Company. This became 'A' Company, 7th Battalion, Bedfordshire and Hertfordshire Regiment.

Tagged with labels, like parcels, these children are evacuees. Separated from their parents, some are confused and frightened. To others it seemed like a great adventure to travel on the train all the way from the South Coast or London to Bedford. How important they must have felt, when they were greeted at the station by the Mayor of Bedford and borough officials. The children in this picture are just some of the thousands to whom the people of Bedford opened their doors and hearts during the years of the war. It was not easy absorbing so many children into the community. the

boys at Owen's School, Islington, shared the buildings of Bedford Modern School. Here they are assembled outside the canteen on the fairground site in Commercial Road. How well organised and well behaved they all seem, as they are given refreshments before going to their new homes. The first evacuees left London on 1 September 1939, two days before war was declared. Bedford gained many grateful friends during the war. As many tears fell when the children had to leave their 'aunts' and 'uncles' and return to their parents, as there had been when they arrived, nearly six years earlier.

For the little boy on the second row it was all too much. He has to cover his eyes. For these evacuees' mums and dads, so far away, are briefly forgotten, as they wait for the raising of the curtain. The fan-fare will soon sound, provided by the mother-of-pearl decorated accordion, and the little blonde girl will be able to return to her seat. The windows are shuttered to prevent the slightest beam of light from escaping out into the night. We want the villain to be on stage, not knocking on the door in the form of an A.R.P. warden during these times of blackout. The lights dim and Cinderella is sitting by the fire with Buttons, who secretly loves her. The world at war outside the hall is now completely forgotten. If the German bombers were to listen carefully they would hear a tremendous shout of, 'He's behind you!' That would be enough to frighten them away on this night in 1940.

Bedford accepted 13,000 women and children evacuated from London and the South Coast, at the outbreak of war in 1939. Many returned to their homes during that period of quiet, called 'the phoney war', from then to the end of April 1940. The German army surprised the world with their 'Blitzkrieg' (lightning war) tactics. Tanks and armoured vehicles, backed by Stuka dive-bombers, swept across Europe towards the English Channel with a speed that took everyone by surprise.

Below: The sound of 'Moaning Minnie', the air-raid siren, has sounded the all clear on 23 July 1942. The Police sergeant strides away from Ford End Road Railway Bridge, no doubt relieved that the raid had not been worse. The workers from W H Allen's turn the corner and head towards the County Theatre. The theatre's flagpole had survived, but the glass and cast iron canopy over the door was severely damaged. Originally built as an auction room in 1891 it was opened as a theatre by Edward Graham Falcon in 1899. Now the Mount Zion Apostolic and Pentecostal Church, it carries a faint but legible sign, not quite obliterated by a coat of paint, telling of days when it was 'The Royal County Theatre Bingo and Social Club. Air Raid Wardens were appointed and trained as early as 1938, at a time when many believed that the war would never happen, or if it did, they thought it would not last very long. The Home Office produced a booklet entitled, 'The Protection of Your Home against Air Raids'. The Air Raid

Warden's began as unpaid volunteers but in 1939 they became paid staff. The small remuneration was not the reason why many of them dealt with incendiary devices, administered first aid, or helped to rescue victims from the rubble of buildings after a raid.

Bottom: 'War Weapons Week' advertised on this poster in St Paul's Square is yet another of the slogans which gave everyone the opportunity to contribute to the 'war effort'. All around the town there were barometers informing the people of Bedford of the progress being made giving a competitive feel to the affair. 'Our boys can't do the job if we don't provide the bullets', was the message. Morale was boosted when there was a feeling that the sacrifices made were having a direct effect in helping husbands, sons, and fathers, and bringing the day when loved ones could return home just a little closer. 'Dig for Victory' was another to which

the people could directly apply themselves. They may have felt helpless at reports of German U-boats sinking the ships which were bringing much needed food, but it made them all the more determined to turn flower beds and any available space into vegetable plots. 'Wings for Victory Week' offered an opportunity to 'buy' a Spitfire for £5,000. The bricks and building materials, stacked by the wall of 1 St Paul's Square, are being used to construct a bomb-blast shelter. Church bells were to be rung in the event of an invasion. The bells of St Paul's Church had been removed at the beginning of the war and were stored in the corner of the churchyard.

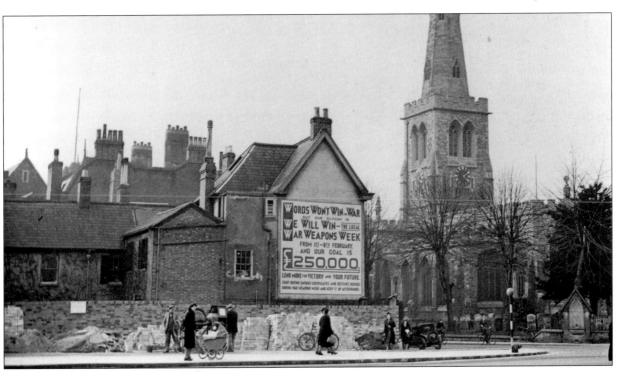

Above: No German paratrooper would dare attack the Peacock (now the Mill) Hotel whilst these lads are on the job. This may only be an invasion exercise on Sunday 6 September 1942, but if determination and resolve were anything to go by, any invader landing in Bedford had better watch out! The 'German' armed forces invaded Britain, and thus followed one of the most realistic mock battles ever staged. Smoke and tear gas were used in this drama, but, as at the pictures, the 'goodies' won!

The Home Guard was formed in May 1940 as the Local Defence Volunteers (LDV). Because most of them were too old to join the regular army, they were affectionately known as 'Dad's Army'. They did not have a uniform or proper weapons at first and on the whole were not taken too seriously by anyone. Many of them worked in reserve occupations. LDV means 'Look', 'Duck' and 'Vanish', was the witty joke of the time. Their name was changed to the Home Guard later in the year and they were properly equipped and given training. When they were linked to local army battalions, their image soon improved. They built pillboxes, removed road signs to confuse the enemy should they land on our shores., dug trenches and manned anti-aircraft rocket batteries.

Above right: Throughout 1942 Civil Defence practice raids continued. The British troops beat off the enemy. They confused the invaders by painting out, or turning all the road signs in the area to disorientate them. The ploy seemed to work every time in these 'battles'. The people needed something to raise their spirits, and, when they visited the cinema, saw the Nazis being thwarted in their evil attempts at world domination. In *Casablanca*, the cynical Rick, played by Humphrey Bogart, regained his youthful ideals when he met the love of his life again. The beautiful Swedish actress, Ingrid Bergman, played his sweetheart. It went some way to making the members of the audience forget that rationing was on the increase. Morale had also received a boost when twenty-six nations signed a 'Declaration of the United Nations' in Washington on the first day of January 1942. In August 1941 Churchill had met President Roosevelt aboard the battleship *Prince of Wales* moored off Newfoundland to sign an Anglo-American agreement, containing eight common principles. It is now better known as The Atlantic Charter. There was other good news. An American pharmaceutical company was mass producing a drug heralded as a 'wonder drug'. It was penicillin, a British discovery.

Each is armed with a bottle of beer and a bread roll; there is a pause for a moment for the camera before the soup is served to these deserving members of the Home Guard at their annual supper in October 1944. Formed as the Local Defence Volunteers in May 1940, they were ill-equipped and a target of many jokes. Music hall comedians had an apparently endless source of jokes. By 1944, however the Home Guard was well-trained, provided with proper uniforms, and equipped ready for any possible invasion from the enemy.

Once the camera shutter has dropped there will be a buzz of conversation, no doubt about the state of the war. There was a great deal to talk about. In June 1944, the D-Day landings on the beaches of Normandy had been successful. Paris had been liberated from the Germans in August. Maybe thoughts turn to lighter matters. 'What do you think about the film studio that has insured Betty Grable's legs for a quarter of a million dollars?' She was the GI's favourite pin-up, and a favourite of many of these men too, no doubt. Earlier in the year the government had made it known that they had plans for a National Health Service. Having had their beer they may sing some of the songs from the new musical by Rodgers and Hammerstein, *Oklahoma*, which had opened in New York in the previous year.

It was VE day and 8 May 1945 had started with rain. Over London there had been a thunderstorm. Forked lightning had flashed across the dark sky. The man, Winston Churchill, who was everyone's hero on this of all days, is reputed to have smiled and said to his secretary, 'Not another war is it?'

The BBC Home Service had announced the 'Victory Programmes' for the day. They would begin with 'Lift up your hearts', at 7.55 am, followed by 'Robinson Cleaver on the Organ' at 10.30am a 'Works concert' at 12 o'clock, and the climax would be 'The Prime-Minister' at 3 o'clock. Crowds that gathered outside in

the streets and squares throughout the country fell silent as the speech was broadcast. They heard how General Jodl had signed an unconditional surrender. Churchill warned the nation that the war in the Far East was not yet over, and we would need to redirect strength and resources. He ended with the words,

'Advance Britannia, Long live freedom, God save the King'. The crowds everywhere erupted in song. Hooters, horns, and in some places bells, sounded, though not here near St Paul's Church, as the bells had been removed at the start of the war and were still stored in the corner of the churchyard.

Bottom: Give these partygoers a wave. Give them the victory 'V' sign. Shout praises for 'Winnie', who had made that sign famous. For these people on this day, Winston Churchill can do no wrong. He will be broadcasting to the nation at 3pm, and no-one will miss that historic speech. Pull up a chair, pull up a table, pull up a piano and join in the celebration. There is David, on the left, wearing his braces. Why did mothers always insist that boys should wear braces and short pants? Who told them it was healthy to walk about with your legs exposed? It's amazing how these myths begin. Many a boy has stood with his arms folded, or has had to wear his Fair Isle tank-top jumper in the hottest weather, in order to hide his embarrassing braces. Joe has taken the fiddle from the shelf and given it a dust. Frank can 'tickle the ivories' almost as well as Charlie Kunz. The drummer had better get in the mood, and play 'In the Mood' soon, or risk being replaced. This party is typical of hundreds held all across the country. A sheer burst of energy and relief. The normal reserve and formalities were dropped, and a close sense of belonging was adopted.

Right: The flags, the people, and even the telegraph pole and the bicycle saddle, are swaying to the music of the accordion as the march proceeds down Dunstable Street in Ampthill on VE day. The adults could be singing, 'There'll always be an England', or 'There'll be blue birds over the white cliffs of Dover',

or even 'Happy days are here again'. The children are just pleased that it is a holiday and the schools are closed. After six long years of war they were ready to let their hair down. Gas masks have been thrown into a corner and it no longer matters if you leave your curtains open at night even with the light on! A cartoon by Vicky showed one man celebrating by leaving all his lights on all the time. Cowls could come off car headlamps. No risk of a fine now. During the 'black-out', there had been many fatal accidents because lights had to be dimmed. Bonfires were stacked ready to burn effigies of Hitler. Potatoes were washed ready to cook in the red embers of the fire. They tasted good, even if it was margarine that was spread over them instead of butter.

seven coupons, and a child's vest took two coupons and a pair of knickers the same. A winter coat took a massive eighteen coupons, so thank goodness that the sun is shining on this day in May, declared a holiday by the government.

Top: The bunting has now dried out from the rain of the previous night on VE day. Chairs have been brought out from the front rooms, and the trestle tables have been borrowed from the church hall. Everyone has contributed as much as they can. Their skills in making cakes using powdered eggs and powdered milk, and very little sugar have been tested to the full. Clean, flowered aprons protect the 'Sunday best' dresses. The kettles are boiling and the Brooke Bond Tea is brewing. Once the photograph has been taken for posterity, the party can get into full swing. At the head of the table is Old Mother Riley, the guest of honour. The children have gathered at that end of the table to be near their heroine (or hero), who always wins against evil every Saturday matinée. Assisted, as she (or he) was, by her (or should it be his?) daughter Kitty, Arthur Lucan played Old Mother Riley, whose daughter Kitty was, in real life, his (or her) wife. Little wonder the children of this era were confused! A banner at the head of Garfield Street welcomes Reg home, but he was one of the lucky ones. Soldiers grew a little impatient over the following months. Because there was still much work to be done in war-torn Europe, demobilisation was a very slow process.

Above: With the fear of war lifted it is good to be British as the family walks along The Embankment. Triumphant flags fly above the former skating rink. No fear of the 'doodlebugs' or the merciless V2 rockets. No need to carry the gasmasks, although these have probably been abandoned for quite some time. After all gasmasks lost all their amusement for most little boys, once they had mastered the trick of making the rubber valve noses vibrate by blowing air down them. Fathers would soon be returning and family life could return to normal once more. Mother has done a good job in his absence. She has had to take government advice and 'Make do and Mend'. Her children also look well attired, smart and well groomed. Quite a feat of management when clothes rationing gave each person only sixty-six coupons per year at the beginning of the war, reducing to forty-eight by Spring 1942. A lady's dress would require eleven coupons, a skirt needed

Left: It was great fun to hang old Hitler from the gas lamp on V.E. Day. Germany had surrendered on 7 May 1945. General Jodl, chief of staff of the German Army, had signed an agreement of unconditional surrender, but the war had really been over for several days. The Russians had taken Berlin and the German forces in the west had already surrendered to Montgomery. They celebrated and sang in anticipation of the end of wartime hardships. This was not to be the case, however, and food and clothing would continue to be in short supply for some years to come. This did not worry these young revellers on this day which had been declared a national holiday. They may have been denied the pleasure of seeing Hitler face the consequences of his actions, since he had shot himself a week earlier, but the sheets stuffed with paper and rubbish are a pretty good likeness and it was a fine feeling to shake your fists at it and say 'Never Again'. The first verdicts in the trials of Nazi war criminals were given on 1 October 1946 at Nuremberg. Although there was little sympathy for the Nazi leaders, the trials caused many legal arguments as their defence was that they were only following Hitler's orders.

Below: Like the cork being let out of a shaken bottle of lemonade, the streets burst into song and dance as soon as Churchill's speech was heard over the radio on VE day. The people chanted, 'We want Churchill', outside the ministry building until he, and members of the cabinet, appeared. It was Churchill they wanted. He was the man of the day. The House of Commons waited for his arrival in the chamber. He was due to make a speech, but he was late because of the crowds which barred his way. The House was packed. The normal reserved control was forgotten, and the whole House erupted with cheers as he entered. When he said the words 'the war in Europe is ended'. MPs threw their papers in the air with further resounding cheers. Such behaviour was unheard of in the House. From there he went to a service of thanksgiving and thence to Buckingham Palace. The King, wearing naval uniform, went out onto the balcony with the Queen and the two Princesses. Crowds were celebrating, singing and dancing beneath them. The people, for whom Churchill could do no wrong on this day, voted him out of office only two months later. A Labour Government, lead by Clement Attlee, was elected in the first general election for ten years. They no doubt thought of all the social reforms, which had been brought into being during, and as a consequence of, the war.

Left: In the words of Lionel Bart's ironic song, 'What's the matter with kids today? Why can't they be like we were, Perfect in every way?' Here is the proof of the 'truth' of that song: patient waiting for the signal to begin. In these days of sugar rationing, the temptation to start must have been great. The ladies have been baking and there are jam tarts, cakes and biscuits. Bowls of jelly, but it will not have banana in it. 'Mummy what is banana?' the children may well ask. With the exception of one little boy, they all pose and 'watch for the birdie'. A credit to their parents and guardians who turned them out looking clean and well-dressed in days when clothes had to be recycled and handed down. If you were the youngest you rarely received new in the days of 'Make Do and Mend'. This party, at the Coventry Road Hall, could be for evacuees or it may be a VE Day celebration. The folding chairs are out, the tables are covered with what tablecloths are available, the church cups and saucers will have to be returned at the end of the day, but it is three o'clock and time to eat. Whatever the occasion, the moment the camera has snapped the picture the noise and laughter will begin.

Above: Once more the parents of children, who live in Coventry Road, have excelled themselves. What fine outfits. It was well worth standing still, high on the chair, whilst mother pinned the costume in place ready for today. Mums and Dads stand admiring their offspring, certain that their child's costume is the best. But no losers on this day in June 1953, everyone is to be a winner, because the Queen is to be crowned. Roy Rogers (without his horse Trigger), a nurse, a sailor, a small Al Jolson, a fairy standing on a chair again, but this time in order to be seen by the camera, will all receive a prize. They will also be given a copy of the New Testament, and a coronation cup to stand on the shelf forever to remind them of this day. They are all fortunate not to be wearing their raincoats or sheltering under an umbrella because the weather has been a little unpredictable and unsea-sonable. A film starring Gene Kelly, is a smash hit in this year of the coronation, *Singing in the Rain*. Everyone remembers the famous dance sequence as Gene Kelly gets a thorough soaking, and the humour of Donald O'Connor. All of this topped off with the voice of the lovely Debbie Reynolds.

Below: Decorations went up throughout Bedford in preparation for the VE day celebrations on Tuesday 8 May. Bunting was stretched across the streets and flags were raised wherever there was a place for them It rained during the night and the bunting sagged a little, but he spirits of the people were buoyant. The gentleman climbing the ladder propped against the wall of the Empire Cinema has regained his youth with the news of an end to hostilities. Inappropriately dressed in a felt hat and suit, he helps to celebrate victory. He was, more than likely, remembering how the street was decorated after the first world war and telling the boys how they did it in 1918. 'We did it better then', he is no doubt saying, 'and we had better films', and clinging to the ladder at that height he is probably remembering the first *Tarzan of the Apes*. Elmo Lincoln played Tarzan, and although the scenery looked more like California than a tropical rain forest, the film was the first of many. It was interesting to see the Union Jack and the Stars and Stripes of America, blowing in the breeze alongside the Hammer and Sickle of Russia. Soon tension would build, Berlin would be divided, and the very same flags would wave on opposite sides of a wall.

Right: It is serious business, down in Mill Meadows, as the balloons rotate above the target. The fellow in charge has no time to consider the rain, because the game, whatever the object of it, is reaching a climax. Do the propellers power the balloons or is the arm, on which they are suspended, powered in some way? Whatever the secret of the machine, it has gathered a crowd. It must be an event of some importance to bring a crowd on such an unpleasant day. It may well be one of the fund raising 'weeks', of which there were many, which were generously supported. The people of Bedford scraped the last few coppers from the back of the drawer, or from down the back of the settee, because it was a way in which they could feel that they were bringing the war a little closer to an end. Perhaps the choice of game gives us a clue that it is 'Wings for Victory' week. Or the balloons could represent torpedoes, rather than airships, and it could be Warship Week'. Airships, like the R101, were built at Cardington, Bedford. It crashed in flames in 1930 with the loss of many lives. With the much recorded and horrific explosion of the German dirigible, *Hindenburg* in 1937 the end of an era was reached.

VE day started quietly, and for many it was a normal working day, despite the declaration that it was to be a public holiday. The Union Jack is flying and the golden bull looks down onto a very subdued High Street at nine o'clock. It seemed an anticlimax in some ways. What did mark the end of a war? The news that the German forces in Italy had surrendered on 2 May 1945, and that Hitler and his wife, Eva Braun, had committed suicide two days earlier was already known. The German army in NW Europe had surrendered to Field Marshal Montgomery on 4 May. For many the end of the war would be marked when their loved ones came home, when rationing had ended, and one no longer had to join a queue in the High street. That day was a few years away yet. The sight of American soldiers, like the one crossing the road in front of the bank, would continue to be a familiar sight. The people of Bedford regarded Glenn Miller as one of them. His bronze bust resides in a niche in the wall of the Corn Exchange where he and his band had entertained with their music. It was placed there in 1994 to commemorate his death 50 years earlier on 15 December 1944. In 1942 his record 'Chattanooga Choo-Choo' sold a million copies, earning him a golden disc.

In many areas VJ Day did not evoke the same
response as VE day had done. Sons and
husbands were still fighting the war against
Japan, after victory was achieved in Europe.
It must have seemed premature, on VE day, to
bring out the tables, lay the clean white cloths
tinged with 'dolly blue' and be lavish with the

rations, whilst any news of their loved ones was
difficult to obtain. But, only a month later, the
Japanese surrendered unconditionally. On 6 and 9
August two Atom Bombs were dropped on
Hiroshima and Nagasaki, with such horrific consequences that the Japanese gave in the fight almost
immediately. To these celebrating and giving the

familiar 'Victory V' sign, the horror of this new form of warfare had not yet been understood. Their only thoughts were of an end to all conflict. For the old lady in the wheelchair much had happened in her lifetime. As she poses for the camera she will remember the turn of the century, when she was in her thirties and the Kodak Company had invented the Brownie Box Camera. She had seen the men go to fight the Boers in South Africa, the Germans in two wars, and now the end of a war against Japan. In her life the first aeroplanes had flown, the telephone had been invented, and now an atom bomb had been dropped. She must be wondering if this was really 'progress'.

Below: With gasmasks abandoned, the young folk gather at the base of the John Howard statue on the Market Square. It is VJ day. Families are strolling through the square with no fear that the siren will sound at any moment and they will have to dash for cover. Life seems good. The boy may well have been wishing for his birthday, when dad and mum will consider him sufficiently old enough for his first pair of long trousers. It was an important step in the 'coming of age' of a chap, but good, responsible behaviour was expected before he was considered 'ready'. Perhaps the young men are discussing

Japan's unconditional surrender. The enormity of it had not yet been realised. Up to 9 August 1945 despite the total destruction of the Japanese Navy, and the near starvation of the Japanese people, Japan would not capitulate, but on that day the second atom bomb was dropped on Nagasaki. The first had entirely destroyed Hiroshima, a name that became a symbol of the unusual destructive power of the atom bomb. Seventy-eight thousand people died instantly, and many thousands more were seriously injured. The effects of radiation were not understood at this time, so the full horror was not yet known.

The bunting was out in many villages in Bedfordshire to celebrate VE Day (Victory in Europe) and VJ Day (Victory in Japan). Here in Lidlington rations were carefully saved to provide this spread. People joined in with their neighbours to enjoy the weather and the end of hostilities. Trestle tables were lifted from the church hall and covered with clean tablecloths. Flower containers were gathered and blooms cut to provide this feast. Folks were growing accustomed to improvising. How smart they all looked as they sat enjoying the sun and the pleasant company. Clothing joined the list of items rationed in 1941 and the ladies were encouraged to 'make-do and mend'. The ladies of the day were ingenious and received useful hints and tips about sewing from public information films throughout the war. But the ladies missed no opportunity, they made undergarments from parachute silk (so we are told), and when they could not get silk stockings they were perfectly willing to colour their legs with gravy browning and add a convincing seam up the back with an eye-brow pencil. Clothes rationing did not end until 1949 when shops held special sales to celebrate, even though the Government warned that they had the power to freeze prices should they rise sharply.

The navy get that sinking feeling on the slide in Mill Meadows. Hopefully they are only posing, for the slide is wet and the nails could well do a 'mischief' to their bell-bottomed trousers. Victory has been won and Churchill is soon to announce the signing of an unconditional surrender by the German forces. It's a great day whatever the weather.

Soon the parties will get into full swing, and, in the words of the song, 'All the nice girls love a sailor', so these likely lads will have partners to dance with tonight. They will be 'bopping' in the streets to the music of that new sensational jazz called 'Be-Bop',

or 'Bop' for short. A leading light in this music is the zany trumpet player, Dizzy Gillespie. There is a strong possibility that, as the evening progresses, they will dance to the rhythm of GlennMiller's 'Moonlight Serenade'.

The previous month had seen the death of President Roosevelt. The press had made comments that he looked frail when the 'big three', Roosevelt, Churchill and Stalin, had met in February at Yalta. They were debating policy to be adopted when the war ended. Roosevelt had attended against medical advice, because he wanted the help of the Russians in the war with Japan.

young men in the crowd will still be called for national service for a long time to come and the ration books will not be abandoned for some time either.

Top: On 11 November 1946 poppies were on sale, but now there were two world wars to remember. Lucky survivors gave willingly in Bedford. The shop windows were still fairly empty. Clement Attlee, Britain's new Prime Minister, brought everyone down to earth with a few common-sense facts, making it clear that it would be several more years before we could stop using dried eggs, or shop for clothes without counting the coupons. The gentleman posing for the camera could well be wearing his 'Demob' suit. Many soldiers,

Above: VE celebrations in the recreation ground. The bonfire is well ablaze casting a comforting glow over people who had not dared shine the smallest light for fear of giving away their position to the enemy above. The enemy below, in the form of the Air Raid Patrol warden, would have brought the weight of the law down on anyone who was showing the smallest chink of light through the front room curtains. Many will remember making screens for the windows out of blackout material. The women folk made good use of any remnants for items of clothing. Many a boy ran the gauntlet of ridicule at school when he had to wear the trousers mum had made from the black cloth. Living-room doors were draped with curtain so that one could open the outer door and leave the house without casting a light. Car and motorcycle headlamps were cowled and gave barely sufficient light through their louvered slots. All this is forgotten now as the children copy Winston Churchill's victory 'V' signal with their fingers. They won't get away with making the same gesture in a few years time. The

demobbed after military service, headed straight for Montague Burton's with the vouchers they had been given. They were dressed from top to toe with 'the full Monty'. America, knowing of the chronic shortages throughout Europe, organised CARE parcels (Co-operative for American Remittances to Europe) containing food and supplies. In 1946 they sent over twelve million tons of grain alone. Flights could now land at the newly opened airport at Heathrow which had replaced the former Croydon airport. Plans were also in operation this year to build yet another at Gatwick. A new, cold and frightening phrase entered the English language. 'The Iron Curtain'. Winston Churchill made a speech in March 1946, in Fulton, Missouri USA, in which he warned that, 'From the Baltic to the Adriatic, an Iron Curtain has descended across the continent'. The west now felt threatened by a hostile power, the Soviet Union. In the first year of peace, however, people did not fully accept the problems, which he clearly foresaw.

Bottom: It was October 1945 when Alderman Canvin, the Mayor of Bedford waited at Midland Road Station, with several anxious relatives, for the repatriated prisoners of war from the Far East. Everyone wants to get into the picture. Although the soldier and the mayor strike a happy pose, there is no controlling the joy and relief of the waiting crowd. Relatives and friends must have been concerned about the health and condition of their loved ones. They had already heard horrific stories about the treatment of prisoners in the concentration camps of Germany, and the prisoner of war camps in Japan, but now their questions and their prayers are answered and the first arrives home. The young man wearing the army boots and cycle clips, clutches his camera, ready to make his own personal record of the event once the official photographer finished.

Only a little over two months earlier Japan had signed an unconditional surrender when the second Atom Bomb had been dropped on Nagasaki. The first was dropped on Hiroshima from an American B-29 bomber, called the 'Enola Gay' after the pilot's mother. The two Japanese cities disappeared in a terrible instant and their names were etched into the pages of our history books for all time. Wars would never be the same again.

Right: We welcomed them back, these brave young men. Mothers waited at the station in Bedford for them to step from the train, wondering what state of health their husbands and sons would be in. These were repatriated prisoners. Stories and pictures had arrived before them of the horrors discovered by the Soviet forces as they entered the concentration camp at Auschwitz and of the atrocities to which prisoners had been subjected elsewhere. We gave the ex-POWs our thanks and a cinema ticket to the Granada. We would have given them anything they asked for. These heroes had given us their limbs, and some had given the full price of their lives.

The film they are about to see could feature Betty Grable, the GIs' favourite pin-up, the blonde 'bombshell' with the beautiful legs. The girls may be swooning in envy as Joan Crawford falls into the arms of that 'heart-throb' Clark Gable. Maybe they could laugh now as George Formby outwitted the spies, and then sang as he was 'Leaning on a lamp-post at the corner of the street in case a certain little lady came by'. They may well agree with him as he winked and said, 'Turned out nice again!'.

Wheels of time

'**D**rivers must not overtake', seems an obvious and unnecessary piece of advice on the Town Bridge before it was widened in 1939. On the right can be seen the corner of the Bank Buildings which was demolished in 1938 in preparation for the bridge alterations. An unbroken white line has clearly marked the road to emphasise the guidance. The white lines were first introduced in 1927. In the same year it became mandatory to have speedometers in cars, and a 30 mph speed limit was imposed in built up areas, which came into force in 1935. From the ending of the 20 mph limit in 1930, until the imposition of the new limit, there were a large number of accidents, many of which were fatal. The drivers of these cars, waiting to cross the bridge, would be glad to achieve the old speed limit. Whilst they queue here on the bridge, they may well be marvelling at the achievements of their hero Malcolm Campbell. He had recently broken the three hundred mile per hour barrier, in his car, *Bluebird*, on Utah Flats in America. Many a boy owned a model *Bluebird* car, powered by a clockwork motor. There was a technique to holding the wheels whilst the spring was fully wound, and not releasing them until the car was aimed in the right direction. Then it would fly across the floor, with greater speed than these motorists are achieving.

'Robotic traffic lights' have now been placed at the busy junction of Mill Street and the High Street. The world's first traffic lights were installed in front of the House of Commons in 1914. No road markings have yet been introduced to keep pedestrians, cyclists, cars and buses in line. No sign either of any 'cats eyes', those rubber studs invented by a Halifax man Percy Shaw in 1934, which could retract when a car went over them, but which shone in the light of headlamps at night to mark the centre of the road. 'The Highway Code' is much needed and 'The Green Cross Code' would be a valuable education for the people captured here on camera. How clear the lessons given to us by 'Green Cross Man' seem even now. 'I won't always be here to see you across the road children, so remember. Never cross between parked cars and keep looking both ways as you cross'.

The increase in traffic in all towns brought about many changes to them. Shortly after this picture was taken in 1937, the double fronted Georgian building, seen here between the bus and car, was demolished. The buildings which replaced it were set back to allow more room for the traffic to negotiate the corner. Taylor, Brawn and Flood, the chemists continued in the new premises. The Cross Keys Inn still remains.

Above: The Broadway in 1927. What a sight for the eyes of any veteran or vintage car enthusiast! Eight cheeky faced Fords all in a row. Some elements of the design of the horse-drawn coaches, from which they descended, can be traced. The oval shape of the rear windows, and their canvas roofs betray that ancestry. The chassis, which still takes the shape of the shafts into which the horse would have been guided, now holds a different power source. Although the poor animal has been super-seded, the replacement is still measured in 'horse-power'. A variety of bodies were built onto the same chassis. The immortal Model T Ford was the first of the 'people's cars'. By 1927 some cars had the luxury of electric starters, but the cranking handle was still an essential piece of equipment. Electric lights fitted as standard had been in existence, along with the starter, since 1911. In 1927 the first London to Brighton Commemoration Run was organised by the *Daily Sketch* newspaper. This annual run is for cars built before 31 December 1904, so these cars are far too modern. It re-enacted the celebratory run made when the 'Emancipation Act' of 1896 ended the rule that a man, carrying a red flag should walk ahead of the car to warn other road users of his approach.

John Bunyan may well be thinking that his pilgrim made easier progress than the traffic, which is on the move beneath him. The policeman on duty is diverting traffic left into Dame Alice Street. Confusion reigns with the introduction of the one-way system in 1965.

Those who have driven a Ford Anglia will remember well this little family car. It had a mechanical windscreen wiper, which slowed and stopped when the engine was straining up hill or away from a stand still, but which suddenly swung wildly when the pressure was taken from the

engine. The sloping rear window caused a minor sensation when the car was first introduced. These cars had many built in comforts such as a heater, placed beneath the dashboard. The heater had a variable speed fan pumping air through a radiator heated by the water from the engine. The temper- ature was controlled by a valve, which stopped the flow of water. The temperature in the car was maintained a little by chance and good fortune. Seat belt anchor points were incorporated into the doorposts and floor. The seat belt law was intro- duced in 1969.

Bottom: Looking smart in their white-topped caps and overalls theses drivers proudly display their comfortable coaches in about 1957. Keen to show the improvements that had occurred since the war, they had an eye on the touring and passenger services that had once been the domain of the now struggling railways. Coach companies throughout the country were quick to realise that the railways could not offer the flexibility which they had. One advantage that the coach offered was the guarantee of a seat. Where coach stations had once been car parks or worse, with conditions underfoot oily and muddy, a new style of architecture had emerged. The two-penny chocolate machine, which rarely delivered the silver wrapped bar, was now replaced by a waiting room and café. They now had ample luggage space on the coaches for the brown leather suitcases, but still advised travellers as to what they thought was an adequate size.

Birch Brothers of London, whose coach terminal was The Broadway, and Beaumonts Coach Service whose coaches left from the Cattle Market, both ran regular daily services from Bedford to London. A single fare was three shillings, or 15p, and a day return cost the princely sum of three shillings and nine pence (nearly 20p). For five shillings and sixpence (27½p) a 'period ticket' could be purchased, with the same guarantee of a seat.

Right: Is the 128 departing from the Broadway Bus Station? Or is it posing for the camera along with the two inspectors, proud now of their more efficient and 'streamlined' buildings and facilities. Whilst there was a steady increase in the number

of privately owned cars, they were still a middle-class commodity and most people relied on the bus to get them about the town. Passengers, however, now demanded a higher standard of service and expected to find a café, newsagent, toilets and other amenities at the bus station. Some even had 'those American style milk bars' which had become fashionable. The bus station in The Broadway was built in 1938 and was replaced by a new one in Greyfriars 22 years later. The prefabrication of metal-framed windows helped bring down the cost. The rounded forms gave a strong sense of style, whilst keeping the expense at a reasonable level.

The Clean Air Act was introduced in 1956, and was to come into force in 1958. No more 'peasoupers'. No more 'smogs', that lethal mixture of fog and smoke. The Government had provided anti-smog masks since 1953, under a doctor's prescription, on Britain's National Health Service.

I t soon became obvious that the bus station was not adequate for the service which was now needed for the town. Much debate was going on in Bedford regarding the possibilities of routes to take traffic away from the centre and ease the congestion. The need for crossings is only too apparent. Crossings received their stripes in 1951 and their beacons flashed a warning to drivers from 1952. Towns like Bedford created pedestrianised areas, which are now such a familiar and pleasant feature of the town, in response to the number of accidents on the roads. In the fifties, although there were many cars about and the

rationing of petrol was at an end, most people still travelled by bus. Many of the cars were pre-war, like the little Austin parked so thoughtfully outside the busy station. Not a single line or traffic warden about to advise him, though there is no doubt that the driver of the bus has some good ideas as to where the driver might park his car! Perhaps it was with this sort of problem in mind that the Government introduced the Highway Code in November 1954. A copy of the code was given to every provisional licence holder, and members of the public could buy one for the handsome sum of one penny.

Bottom: Things which can never be captured on film, are the noise, the smells, and the feeling of the sheer power of a steam locomotive. They were sooty, and hissed steam into the air, but that animated them and gave them a life that endeared them to us. They achieved great feats and made us wish to name them. The 4472 was known to every schoolboy at the height of the period of steam locomotives. It was given six different numbers in its lifetime, but there was no mistaking this train because it was 'The Flying Scotsman'. First known as 'The Special Scotch Express' it is not clear when it changed to being 'The Flying Scotsman', but it happened when it was bought from the Great Northern Line by the L.N.E.R. In 1928 it went non-stop from Kings Cross to Edinburgh. It pulled eight twelve wheeled cars carrying passengers in comfort. The picture was probably taken in the early sixties when it had a Pullman refreshment coach added (fourth coach from the front). It broke all records of the time and children and train-spotters would wait eagerly for a glimpse of it when they knew it was due to pass. In January 1963 the train was bought by Alan Pegler who took it to America. At that time it had already logged two million and eighty thousand miles. Ten years later a new owner, W.H.McAlpine, brought it back to England.

Right: By the mid-fifties the railways were showing signs of serious decline. Road, rather than rail, was attracting new traffic. Roads had improved, petrol rationing was at an end, and people were realising that a family car was within their means. New cars were being designed with this group in mind. Alex Issigonis, who had been successful with the Morris Minor ten years earlier, had now come up with the fabulous 'Mini'. It came on sale in August 1959, at a cost of £496.19s.2d. In the same year this DMU rolled into Bedford station powered by a Rolls Royce diesel engine. Although it sported the green livery and 'whiskers' of the Midland Railway, it would not attract the keen railway enthusiasts as its steam-powered grandfather had done. No more steam engines were built after 1960. The government's rescue plan for the railways had begun in 1955 with an injection of over £1.6 billion. The scheme was to cover a period of fifteen years, but had come too late. The M1 motorway opened in this same year, 1959, and bus operators were quick to exploit the advantages of speeds now possible. Although not able to equal the speed of the railway, they could offer much lower fares.

At the shops

A family concern with a branch in Bedford for many years, Grimbly Hughes and Company advertise a store with 'quality and service' in an age when one waited patiently for one's turn to be served. It was a pleasant experience being served with respect. The concept of 'self service' had not been established. When it was first introduced, the idea of taking things off the shelves themselves made many uncomfortable. It felt almost like stealing. They were not accustomed to putting anything into a basket until it had been weighed or wrapped, paid for, and handed to them. For many years the corner shop resisted the advance of the supermarket because it offered that service which Grimbly Hughes so proudly advertise at 73 High Street. The bus stop is situated very close to the traffic lights at the end of Silver Street and could cause some problems on a busier day than this in the early fifties. The lady and her bicycle are under threat from the bus as it turns to come down Silver Street. Grimbly Hughes was demolished in 1957 and replaced by Alexandre, men's outfitters, which is now a toyshop.

John Howard looks down on the people of Bedford as they go about their twice weekly shop on the Market Square. He has done so since he was first unveiled on 28 March 1894 to stirring music played by the Volunteer Fire Brigade Brass Band. The statue commemorates the centenary of the great prison reformer's death. He died in Russia in 1790. He is depicted wearing riding clothes by the sculptor Alfred Gilbert, who is perhaps best known for his statue of Eros, in London. The base of the statue was once a part of a fountain that stood near this spot. It was removed in 1880, but the steps were subsequently re-used for the statue of John Howard. He has stood pensively gazing on High Street and seen the development of the motorcar, and watched as workmen erected a large Parking sign at his base. He must have been delighted, if statues can be delighted, when Bank Buildings were demolished giving him a better view of the bridge widening, and all the other changes as a consequence of the motorcar. He watched the design of the road signs change to the continental style in 1965, and was grateful for the yellow stripes, which stopped cars from parking in front of him.

brake lights were not yet compulsory. Direction indicators of the swinging arm pattern were still fitted to many vehicles. They would stick and required the driver to bang the door column to release them. It was not guaranteed that the light would come on in inside the orange plastic covers, when they did eventually rise.

Top: Marks and Spencer stands on the site where the White Horse Inn once stood. Although concerned about its image with younger people in recent years, M&S has continued to be a popular store with the many

Above: Market day again, with more to buy now that the war and rationing have ended, providing you have the money. The decade had begun with a strong sense of optimism and anticipation of growing prosperity. Pedestrians, on their way to the Market Square, could cross the road in greater safety with the introduction of a 'zebra' crossing in 1951. Although the car was still a luxury item, and many relied on pedal power, attitudes were changing and a family car was within reach of a greater number of people. The bridge had been widened to cope with the growing number, but one-way traffic in the High Street would soon be under consideration. These were the days when cars were in that state of transition from a chassis built design, to a sleeker plan with aerodynamics in mind. The Standard car, with the easily recognised 'fastback' body, had appeared as early as 1947. The more efficient disc breaks were not yet available on most cars, and the tyre laws had yet to come into force. Drivers had to watch with care for signs that the car in front was stopping as

customers who have grown to accept the quality of the goods on sale. The store has offered good customer service throughout its long history of trading. Next-door is the well-known shoe shop, Freeman Hardy Willis. Remember the little dog with the sad face that advertised Hush Puppies on TV, and the Tuf shoes that became fashionable? The thick-soled 'beetle-crushers' to go with the velvet collared jacket and drainpipe trousers, which no self-respecting 'Teddy Boy' would be seen without? The later 'Mods' wore the 'winkle-pickers', with sharp pointed toes, to complement the Italian style suit. Over the years Freeman Hardy Willis must have supplied them all.

The junction of Harpur Street, Silver Street and Midland Road has seen many changes up to the present day. Most of them have been brought about because of the increase in traffic and the need to consider the comfort and safety of the shopper. The cameraman must have been out bright and early on a Sunday morning to find this corner so quiet.

here have been many changes in Bedford brought about by the invention of the motorcar. It has dictated the direction one can travel. Now the movement is one way down the High Street in the direction of the Town Bridge. Yellow lines have appeared to avoid any interruption to the flow of the traffic. Strangers will pass beneath John Howard's statue several times as they try to find a parking place before visiting the market. If the statue could speak, what would he say about the short skirts? Is he in pensive mood as he tries to put his thoughts into words? Mary Quant opened a boutique (before the sixties it would have simply been 'a clothes shop') in London and influenced the world of fashion with her radical ideas. The flowered patterns, to be found on the shirts of men as well as the blouses of women, were symbolic of the new freedoms of the times. Some things gladly remain the same. The cries of the stallholders, singing out to the shoppers. The smells of the fruits and flowers have not changed, and by the sixties they are in plentiful supply and the people have enough money in their pockets to buy them.

More Memories of **BEDFORD**

Summer in the sixties, and the market is in full swing with vendors' cries and plenty on the stalls to satisfy the Bedford shoppers. 'You've never had it so good'; Harold MacMillan had told the people three years earlier. Isn't it strange that we only regard times as the best years of our lives when we look back on them and not when we are living them? The sixties was a decade of contrasts, America elected the youngest president ever, JFKennedy, who was assassinated after three short years, and Berlin's wall was built, dividing east from west. The wall went up, and so did hemlines. The 'mini-skirt' was a sensation when Mary Quant first introduced it, both here and in America. The first British number plates to carry a suffix were introduced in 1963. In 1967 the letter 'E' was used, but changed to 'F' in August. In the same year it became mandatory for all new cars to be fitted with seat belts although it was left to the discretion of the driver as to whether or not they were worn. The Anglia waits to drive onto the road as two cars pass. The Beetle and the Hillman Imp. Rear-engined, rear-wheel drive, they were extremely light on the steering. Anyone who drove them would put something heavy in the boot, which was at the front in both cars, to keep the front wheels pressed down, whenever there was any ice or snow.

Earning a living

No dustbins for these men in 1942. The old tin bath has just found another purpose. There was a day when it would have been lifted from its hook in the cellar on bath night, placed in front of the coal fire, and filled with kettles of hot water. If you were the youngest you were probably last into the water. Mother would top it up with another kettle full to maintain the temperature and then begin to scrub. No consideration was given for the modest, but, 'cleanliness is next to Godliness', we were told.
This picture of wartime salvage collection was taken outside 26 Mill Street.

During the war the same tin baths, saucepans (for the scarce aluminium), and kettles would be sacrificed for the war effort. In fact the truth was that the pots and pans yielded very little high-grade aluminium, but the boost to morale made one feel that a real contribution was being made. 'Every scrap shortens the Scrap', the government propaganda cried. Lord Beaverbrook urged everyone throughout the country to gather scrap, and many returned from an evening at the cinema to discover that their railings had been taken. During 1942, the Ministry of Works gathered 1.5 million tons of scrap, which included 42,000 tons of railings and gates.

Bedford Modern School, looking to the future based securely on history and tradition

In 1764, control of the Bedford Charity passed from Bedford Borough Council to the Harpur Trust, and the Writing School, teaching the important business skill of copper-plate handwriting, was established on the ground floor of the Grammar School (now the Old Town Hall) in St Paul's Square. Rapidly rising rents from the development of the Charity's 13 acres in Holborn, London, enabled the Trust to build new premises in Harpur Street. These were to house the Writing School, an orphanage, a board room and clerk's house, and an elementary school, all behind a splendid Tudor Gothic facade, designed by Edward Blore. The Grammar School stayed in the original building in St. Pauls Square until 1892 when it moved to what is now Bedford School.

The Writing School, renamed the English School following the move, became the Commercial School in mid-century, and finally Bedford Modern School (BMS) in 1873, after a Harpur Trust re-organisation scheme. The scheme also provided for Bedford High School and Girls' Modern School (since renamed Dame Alice Harpur School), both opened in 1882. BMS flourished under Dr R B Poole (Headmaster 1877-

1900) who added new buildings, including science laboratories, and installed electricity. From that time until the end of the Second World War, Bedford attracted many colonial and military personnel seeking good, inexpensive education for their young families. Many OBMs helped to administer the British Empire, and others went into the professions or local businesses. The School Field at Clarendon Street was laid out in 1884 and the BMS cadet corps was founded in its present form in 1900.

C W Kaye (Headmaster 1901-16) built new classrooms and a gymnasium. The Headship of A C Powell (1916-23) was overshadowed by the First World War. A memorial hall behind the Blore Tower commemorated the 167 OBMs who were killed. Headmaster H W Liddle (1922-46) converted Kaye's gym into Big School (the hall) in 1929. A covered swimming-bath was built at the Clarendon Street Field in 1935, and the New Field in

Below: *Rugby football was introduced to BMS by Dr R B Poole (Headmaster 1877-1900), who was educated at Rugby School. This photograph of the 1st XV was taken outside the School Pavilion c.1895.*

Houses named after famous Old Bedford Modernians (OBMs): three scientists (Prof. E T Bell, Sir Charles Oatley, and Sir William Tilden), an empire-builder (Sir George Farrar), a soldier-sportsman (Edgar Mobbs DSO), and an historian (Prof. J Holland Rose), which makes an appropriate representation of OBM achievement. BMS now educates 236 boys in the Junior School from the age of 7, with an enriched curriculum including modern languages, technology, IT and many other activities, and nearly 900 senior boys from 11-18 with a rigorous, differentiated curriculum

Clapham Road was acquired in 1938. A memorial alcove for the 126 OBMs who died in the Second World War, each of whom has a photograph in a book of remembrance, was added in 1948. The war memorials were transferred to the present School site in 1974.

Mr Liddle helped foster adult education and welfare programmes, admitted a number of Jewish boys fleeing Hitler's Germany to the school, and was quick to offer to share the BMS buildings with Owen's School (Islington) in 1939. His successor, the Rev J E Taylor (1946-65) made academic success (mainly Oxbridge entrance) the top priority, built a new science block and found space to enlarge the school library and offices by persuading the Harpur Trust to transfer the School Museum (1886), with its archaeological and local history collections, to the borough council to become the nucleus of Bedford Museum, opened in 1962.

Under Headmaster B H Kemball-Cook (1965-77), BMS moved to its purpose built present site in Manton Lane in 1974, whilst the old school was redeveloped as the Harpur (shopping) Centre behind the preserved Blore facade. He liber-alised the regime, expanded the curriculum, and welcomed the Queen and Prince Philip in 1976. At this time BMS became independent after nearly sixty years as a direct grant school. Consolidation and improvement have marked the last twenty-five years at BMS, with new buildings for design and technology, the Robert Luff Sixth Form Centre, and a rebuilt swimming bath, all under P J Squire (1977-96).

Throughout an era of continuous modernisation, essential BMS traditions have been maintained. Under Headmaster Stephen Smith (appointed in 1996), the House system has been reorganised. There are six

appealing to both the gifted boy and the good all-rounder. Great emphasis is placed on pastoral care through a system of year group tutors. Each year group has its own common room. The school, with adjacent playing-fields, offers modern facilities and further expansion is being planned.

In response to significant parental demand for family-based education in one school, BMS is looking forward to welcoming girls in September 2003, subject to a feasibility study, the outcome of which is imminent.

BMS has produced outstanding sportsmen, including cricketers such as A O Jones, who captained the MCC in Australia in 1907-08, rugby players like Dickie Jeeps CBE, who became chairman of the Sports Council, and oarsmen, most notably Tim Foster MBE, Gold Medallist in the men's coxless fours at the Sydney Olympic Games in 2000. A current pupil has been selected to row in the Great Britain under-18 squad. Pre-eminent among literary OBMs is the poet and playwright Dr Christopher Fry, holder of the Queen's Gold Medal for Poetry and the Benson Medal of the Royal Society of Literature. There have been several OBM humorists, from the *Punch* cartoonist G L Stampa, Sir Henry Bashford (author of *Augustus Carp Esq*) and the broadcaster Gillie Potter, to the actor John Sessions. There can be no doubt that a Bedford Modern School education will continue to nurture achievement in every sphere of activity.

Top left: *A woodwork class being conducted by Mr P G Blackburn c.1912 Mr Blackburn taught at BMS from 1908 to 1946.* ***Above:*** *In the centre of the Blore Facade (completed 1833) of the old BMS is the Tower. Left, the bay-window of the Harpur Trust boardroom. Right, the bay-window of Big School (Mr Liddle's school hall).*

Building a university on strong foundations

Being classified as a 'university town' confers an unmistakable status, something clearly lacking in those places which are not host to centres of academic excellence.

De Montfort University in Bedford dates from only 1994 when two of the town's former Colleges merged with the existing university.

Of course in the minds of Bedford's residents such technical niceties are immaterial; we all know that our parts of the University are far older than that.

In fact those parts are even older than most realise. Perhaps some memories will only go back as far as 1976 when Bedford College of Higher Education was formed with the merger of Mander College with the Polhill and Lansdowne Colleges.

The roots of the present University however go far deeper in Bedford. One root can be traced back to the local kindergarten movement which began in the town in the 1850s, although it was not until 1881 that the idea of founding a combined kindergarten school and training college was first mooted and which would soon lead to the establishment not only of a kindergarten but to the foundation of Bedford Training College for Teachers.

The Bedford Kindergarten opened its doors in January 1882 at 34 Bromham Road with 15 pupils in attendance and two months later with 50 pupils in tow it moved to 14 The Crescent.

For the trainee teachers in those days however, the only qualification they received at the end of their studies was the 'Bedford Certificate' after spending anything from one to five years of a somewhat fluid and uncertain curriculum capped by a decidedly generous marking system.

In 1896 a branch school, Froebel House, was opened in Goldington Avenue and in 1899 Shenstone Lodge was acquired as the headmistress's residence and accommodation for young lady students. Two years later the fledgling college was bought out from its charitable trust by its headmistress Miss Walmsley for £2,000.

*Top left: Amy Walmsley, Principal of Bedford Training College from 1896 to 1927. **Above right:** A study in Shenstone Lodge, 1905. **Left:** 37 Lansdowne Road, 1905. **Below:** Number 14 The Crescent, circa 1955.*

The Bedford Physical Training College, another strand in the De Montfort story, was founded in 1903 at Wylam Lodge - now better known as 37 Lansdowne Road.

The physical training college was the result of fashionable Swedish ideas that girls as well as boys should get a healthy physical as well an academic education in order to achieve that ideal of a healthy mind in a healthy body.

Both these early educational institutions catered only for young women. Polhill, as the kindergarten college would become, delayed admitting men to its lecture rooms until 1968 whilst, astonishing as it now seems, Lansdowne delayed admitting male students teachers until the early 1980s.

For both colleges the years between the first and second world wars were ones of expansion, continuing

Top left: The same room in Shenstone Lodge from the previous page in its guise as a Common Room in 1955.
Above left: The library at Polhill pictured in the 1970s.
Above right: Students demonstrating their support for the merger with De Montfort University, 1993.
Right: One of the first graduation ceremonies after the merger, playwright Christopher Fry is awarded the honorary degree of Doctor of Letters by the university's Chancellor, Dame Anne Mueller, September 9th 1994.

independence and increasing repute with state recognition for examinations and consequently a more formal curriculum being part of that process.

During the second world war Lansdowne students were involved in canteen work and work for the Land Army. But for many students at both colleges wartime meant, more than anything else, huddling over a small stove trying to keep warm. Keeping clean could be a problem too since only one bath with a maximum three inches of water was allowed per week.

The ending of the war led an upsurge in the demand for teachers but the two colleges were far from secure, capital to effect repairs and new building was lacking and the idea of, what were in effect, private collages was beginning to seem anachronistic; local authority grants for students to study in non state colleges were harder to come by and were affecting the colleges' incomes badly.

In August 1952 Lansdowne, like The Crescent, gave in to the inevitable and became a maintained college under the control of Bedfordshire County Council. In 1976 that association became closer when the two colleges came together with Mander College of Further Education to form Bedford College of Higher Education until, in 1994, they both left the control of the County Council to become the Lansdowne and Polhill campuses of the De Montfort University. And so at last Bedford became a university town and the story which began there in 1882 with the opening of a kindergarten school had reached its long awaited conclusion.

The information for this story was taken from Richard Smart's book 'On Others' Shoulders'.

Phoenix at Bedford School

Bedford School has seen many centuries. Certainly of ecclesiastical origin it was rescued after the monastic dissolutions and, through Letters Patent of King Edward the Sixth in 1552, was endowed with land in London by Sir William Harper - a native of Bedford, Lord Mayor of the City of London and now regarded as the School's 'Founder'.

Like most Tudor foundations it had good and less good times. But by the nineteenth century it was flourishing, as one of England's notable Public Schools. By 1891, it had outgrown its Tudor buildings and moved to its present Estate, north of the town centre. Its great new buildings were regarded as a marvel by townspeople, and within them it grew in numbers, in national and world influence, and in educational innovation. Here Roentgen Rays were used before 1900, Science was on the curriculum while Victoria was alive, an observatory was open to townsfolk, boarding houses recruited from the families of the Empire and boys were sent to the ancient Universities, the Army and Navy and the Imperial Civil Service. Both wars took their toll: in World War I, 472 boys were killed across all theatres of the war and by 1945 five VCs had been won and the school had been singled out for thanks by Montgomery of Alamein for providing senior military staff. In sporting, musical and intellectual activity the pace was strong and the school was able to compete with the best in Britain. From it came Paddy Ashdown, the essayist H.H.Munro (Saki), novelist John Fowles, an Astronomer Royal, Professors at Oxford and Cambridge, Bishops, a

Vice Chancellor of Cambridge, a Nobel Prize winner, a holder of the Lenin Peace Prize, Governors of the Empire, an Admiral of the Fleet and First Sea Lord, an Air Chief Marshal and Generals too many to list. There were broadcasters, politicians, medical and financial giants; and there were their teachers, of course. It was proving a strong century.

Thus it was, until one night in 1979.

At 11.58pm on Saturday 3 March the first of thirty six emergency calls was received: there was a fire at Bedford School. Some fire. Flames were reported reaching 130 feet into the sky, two fire engines became eighteen, and the glow could be seen from Barton-le-Clay near Luton. It was the biggest and most costly fire to have occurred in peacetime in the county. It was not extinguished until early on the Monday morning. There are descriptions of avalanches of tiles and exploding glass, stone and brick, incandescent copper and a heritage disappearing in flames.

It was a major spectacle and, for many, too much. A resident remembered being 'involuntarily drawn to join others in sharing the agony of helplessness in seeing something precious destroyed before our eyes'. 'The sense of shock, horror and disbelief was quite remarkable'. A boy wrote 'there were five of us in the dorm' and we got up and went to the window and there was the most terrible sight I have ever seen in my life'. Another described 'there really was no

Below: *The devastating fire of March 1979.*

feeling of elation at the sight or consequences. It was a sensation of unreality which was to last for many months until one became accustomed to the new status quo ... .the pre-fabs and English lessons in the pavilion'. 90 per cent of the building was destroyed; 30 classrooms were lost. The story was on the ITN news, and in the national press on the Monday.

The agony was brought to a conclusion at a 1981 Restoration Concert in the new Great Hall: a specially commissioned work by John Tavener ('Risen') was performed by the boys and Sir George Thalben-Ball played the new organ. Lord Home of the Hirsel later unveiled a plaque commemorating what had happened.

What had happened, of course, was both an agony and an ecstasy. Like a phoenix a new school rose from the embers. The leadership of its Head Master, Ian Jones, set the tone and was an inspiration to staff and boys: on the entrance gates after the fire was a Head Master's notice reading 'Normal school on Monday March 5 at 9.00am'. Not a single teaching period was lost. The new building was a revelation - designed by Sir Philip Dowson, soon to be President of the Royal Academy, it provided a high-tech interior within its Victorian frame. Now

there was a grand concert hall, full audio-visual facilities, newly created accommodation in the old roof space, adequate secretarial and staff rooms, and a quality of craftsmanship and materials which will stand the test of time.

It is now twenty years since the re-opening. The School has indeed 'Risen'. There have been two subsequent 'development programmes' which have produced a theatre, swimming pool and Recreation Centre, a new Preparatory School with its own Erskine-May Hall, Design Technology facilities on an enviable scale, IT suites for boys; and all the boarding Houses have been refurbished. A third development now looks to a new Music School and an innovative Library and Resources Centre. Computers are everywhere and all boys are IT literate. Drama and Music and Art flourish as never before, entry to the Universities of Oxford and Cambridge are at historically high levels (16 last year), and the school's reputation in sport is national and international, as it always had been.

For all Bedfordians, whether of town or gown, the 'Great Fire' was one of the unforgettable memories of the century. For the School it clearly acted as a stimulant which would confirm it as one of the great educational providers in the country.

Above centre: The Gala Concert, 1981.
Top: The school today.

Under the Hammer

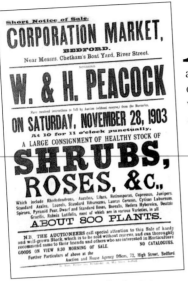

Short Notice of Sale.

CORPORATION MARKET,
BEDFORD.
Near Messrs. Chetham's Boat Yard, River Street.

MESSRS

W. & H. PEACOCK

Have received instructions to Sell by Auction (without reserve) from the Nurseries

ON SATURDAY, NOVEMBER 28, 1903

At 10 for 11 o'clock punctually.

A LARGE CONSIGNMENT OF HEALTHY STOCK OF

SHRUBS,
ROSES, &C.,

Which include Rhododendrons, Aucubas, Lilacs, Retinosporas, Cupressus, Junipers, Standard Azalea, Laurels, Standard Viburnums, Laurus Cerasus, Cytisus Laburnum, Spireas, Pyramid Pear, Dwarf and Standard Roses, Borealis, Hedera Hybernica, Deutzia Gracilis, Rolmis Latifolia, most of which are in various Varieties, in all

ABOUT 800 PLANTS.

N.B. THE AUCTIONEERS call special attention to this Sale of hardy and well-grown Stock, which is to be sold without reserve, and can thoroughly recommend same to their friends and others who are interested in Horticulture
GOODS ON VIEW 9.30 MORNING OF SALE.   NO CATALOGUES.
Further Particulars of above at the
Auction and House Agency Offices, 72, High Street, Bedford

Alongside the ancient custom of bartering an auction sale is one of the oldest ways of buying and selling. The atmosphere in an auction room is like no other. The feeling of anticipation, the sense of controlled excitement and the beating of the heart when the sale of the desired item comes nearer can be a nail biting experience.

However the hustle and bustle of a busy sale room can also be a daunting experience for the newcomer. After all, buying from an auction sale is completely different from popping into a shop or supermarket.

One of the first rules is always to view what you want to buy first and decide how much you are willing to spend - and stick to your financial limit - but it is not always easy; one can get carried away with the excitement.

W&H Peacock Auctioneers have been part of the Bedford business community for a century. From its salesrooms situated in the heart of the town the firm attracts buyers from all over East Anglia and beyond.

The business was started by Walter Molesworth Peacock 1901. In December 1899, inspired by calls for men to serve Queen and country, Walter had attended his employer's, Stafford, Rogers and Merry's, Christmas fat stock sale then joined 'Compton's Horse' for the war in South Africa. When Walter returned from South Africa after two years spent fighting in the

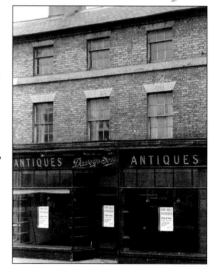

Above left: *An early advertisiement for one of the firm's auctions, this one dating from 1903.*
Right: *Chattel auction sale at Davey's Antiques, St Peters Street, February 1970.*
Below: *Robert Peacock on the rostrum, flanked by Dudley Peacock.*

Boer War it was to find that his job at the livestock auctioneering firm of Stafford, Rogers and Merry no longer existed. In a fit of righteous indignation he vowed to start his own firm of auctioneers to rival that of his former employers. The record shows how well he succeeded.

Since its genesis in 1901 Peacock's has evolved taking on other names including TSB in 1988 which eventually became Lloyds TSB and thus for a time placing the firm under the Black Horse Agency's umbrella. A subsequent commercial move would see ownership fall to the Bradford and Bingley chattel auction business. In the latest twist in the history of Peacock's Bradford and Bingley last year sold to its own management team. The new amalgamated group would form one of the largest independent provincial auction businesses in Britain employing over sixty staff and selling around 5,000 lots every week from four auction centres in the Midlands, East Anglia and the south east.

The new company continues to trade under the existing names of Locke and England in Leamington Spa, Warwickshire, Ambrose in Loughton, Essex - but in Bedford and St Neots Cambridgeshire the firm has reverted to the original name of W&H Peacock.

And the jewel in the W&H Peacock crown is undoubtedly the Auction Centre. This 22,000 square foot building makes it amongst the largest covered auction rooms in the country. The ground floor auction area is divided into four rooms which allows four auctioneers to sell simultaneously at the weekly Saturday sales. On a typical Saturday in excess of 2,000 items are auctioned ranging from a Land Rover to a dozen eggs. The weekly sale is regarded by many townspeople as the best free show in town and as much a part of Saturday as a visit to the supermarket.

---

30 THE EMBANKMENT BEDFORD

CATALOGUE

OF THE

ANTIQUE AND MODERN FURNITURE

To be sold by Auction on the premises by

═ W. & H. ═

PEACOCK

for the Owner, having sold the property
on **TUESDAY, 27th JUNE, 1961**
at 11 o'clock

On View Monday, 26th June—10 a.m. to 4 p.m.

Auctioneers' Offices
10 LIME STREET, BEDFORD
(Telephone: 66366)
6 DAME ALICE STREET, BEDFORD
and BALDOCK and KNEBWORTH

Henry Burt & Son Ltd, Mill Street, Bedford

Above centre: *Another advertisement, this one from the 1960s.*
Top: *The front yard at Horne Lane on a busy Saturday morning.*

Back in 1901 however when Walter set up his new business as auctioneer, estate and land agent he did so from the High Street conducting auction sales initially from Commercial Road and later in Horne Lane (which became the Howard Centre). The first sale was held in the Bedford cattle market in September 1901.

The name W&H Peacock did not appear until April 1902 when Walter was joined by his brother Harry. The

following year, 1903, they commenced sales at Lime Street Auction Rooms.

In 1906 the firm opened offices at 84, High Street. Ten years later during the first world war in 1916 Peacock's began holding sales in the Front Yard and Poultry Yard in Horne Lane.

Following the 'war to end all wars' in 1906 offices at 10, Lime Street were opened for accounts.

Until the late 1950s both Peacock brothers continued to take an active part in the business holding open air sales of livestock such as hens, day-old chicks, pet rabbits and even ferrets.

In 1921 Walter's son Robert M Peacock joined the firm and would eventually become its longest serving member of staff.

Above: *Lime Street offices and 'The Rooms' auction room.* ***Top:*** *Horne Lane, saleyard.*

In 1923 sales began in the Furniture Yard and two years later the main auction office moved from 84, High Street to join the accounts office in Lime Street.

An estate agency office at 6, Dame Alice Street had opened in 1928 whilst the auction and agricultural office and furniture salesrooms were relocated to Lime Street. An illustrated property guide issued by Peacocks in the 1930s makes interesting reading when one compares house prices to the present day. Back then one could buy a four-bedroomed house with two recreation rooms for just £525. Or even a seven bedroomed house for less than a thousand pounds.

Out in the countryside £2,000 would buy a 'Charming residence in a lovely position overlooking pine woods. Modern house on two floors only, containing hall, three reception rooms, kitchen, scullery, usual offices, five bedrooms, separate WC, garage, two stall stables, tennis courts, conservatory and almost an acre of land.' Those were the days!

The Dame Alice Street office would remain open for 36 years before eventually closing in 1964, a year which also saw other major changes when Robert and Dudley Peacock were joined in partnership by Messrs. Jeffrey, Knights and Lazenby.

Further amalgamation would occur in the 1970s when Peacocks - by then W&H Peacock, Bedford, Baldock and Knebworth - merged with Western & Co. When Horne Lane was redeveloped in 1977 Peacock's moved to its new 22,000 sq. ft Newnham Street site.

In 1978 the antique sales finally moved from Lime Street to the first floor Robert Room (named after Walter Peacock's son) in Newnham Street.

The boom in auction sales and an interest in antiques, particularly over the last two decades, has been fuelled in part by greater affluence, but also by the sheer sameness of modern goods mass produced by the tens and hundreds of thousands on factory production lines - people today more than ever before value uniqueness and quality . Interest has been further fuelled by television programmes such as the long running Antiques Road Show and Going for a Song - not to mention the more recent Great Antiques Hunt which has featured Peacock's.

Television appearances apart the working life of an auctioneer is far from boring. Some very strange

Above: Walter and Harry Peacock.
Below: Newnham Street Auction Centre.
Below left: Mr Kinsey and friend at Horne Lane.

items have landed up at the auction centre over the years - not the least being a coffin.

'What is an antique' is a question which is often raised with Peacock's. The old definition of antique was something made before 1830, before industrialisation began to seriously change our surroundings. The official definition of antique however, is 'more than a hundred years old'. But for the general public all kinds of objects such as those in the Art Nouveau style (1880-1914) and Art Deco (1920-40) are eagerly and sometimes expensively collected.

Post war objects are now beginning to make their appearance in shops and sale rooms. In fact the immediate past is to many people more absorbing than any period of history.

Indeed the whole concept of objects worth collecting has changed out of all recognition. Antiques no longer include only the old classic genres of furniture, pottery and porcelain, glass, silver, coins and ethnographica. Today people collect anything under the sun.

Staff never know from day to day what they will come across and there is always an air of expectancy when something very old or unusual is received. And people seem to hide money in the strangest places.

Once when examining a chest of drawers staff found a secret drawer containing hundreds of pounds. But outside valuations also come up with some remarkable finds. A penny farthing bicycle was found hidden behind a pile of boxes, a Roman marble bust was once discovered hidden in a garden shed - which later sold for £2,600-whilst a 1934 Austin 7 stored in a stable reached £3,400 in the sale.

In 1996 the company took over Shaw & Son which has a 12,000 sq. ft site in St Neots. Shaw's too

was a long established firm with roots going back to the reign of Queen Victoria. Chartered surveyor and auctioneer Len Shaw and local businessman Joe Huckle first opened their doors for business in 1924. Inside their New Street auction rooms and yard the partnership of Huckle & Shaw Auctioneers and Valuers continued a tradition first established in the same premises in 1863.

In its early days Huckle & Shaw was primarily an egg packing station with a brisk trade in poultry and vegetables. The successful partnership continued until 1955 when the name outside the premises changed to L Shaw and Son.

John Shaw continued the work his father had started becoming sole proprietor when Mr Shaw senior died in 1966.

But how does one become an auctioneer? One does not need any specific academic qualifications but you do need to be fast. When an auctioneer starts a sale he checks four things: the lot number, its description, the vendor's instructions and lastly the value of any commission bids - that is those sent in by potential buyers who cannot attend the sale of which there may be several.

Armed with this information the auctioneer handles bids from the floor and this is where speed becomes of the essence. A normal sale at Peacock's involves an average 2,500 lots - and on busy days the total can exceed 3,000 - so each sale takes on average just 30 seconds.

Most auctioneers start work on the ground floor, both literally and metaphorically on portering and handling the clerical work.

When the prospective auctioneer is considered capable of handling a sale he is thrown in at the deep end - and told just hours before the auction is due to start.

Above: *Always inspect a lot before you bid!*

According to old hands this is the only way: one cannot go to college to learn this trade. The next step up the ladder for an auctioneer is to become a valuer - and this is very much dependant upon experience, with even those who have been in the trade for decades readily admitting that they are still learning all the time.

The Peacock family has always been involved with the company; up until 2000 Mr Dudley

Above: A busy Saturday auction in Newnham Street.
Top: Dudley Peacock on the rostrum.

Peacock, Walter's grandson, who had joined the firm in 1951, was still paying an active part in the firm.

Naturally W&H Peacock, in common with many other businesses, has experienced some changes over the years, not least being computerisation of the accounts department which processes hundreds of invoices every Saturday.

But what has not changed is the ethos laid down by Walter Peacock more than a century ago - to retain a friendly family atmosphere where the people of Bedford can come to buy or to sell. Perhaps the only difference between those days and now is that the firm's reputation extends far beyond the boundaries of Bedfordshire and attracts people from far and wide.

In the meantime those tempted to attend an auction for the first time just need to observe a few simple rules: when your lot comes up enter the bidding early, don't be nervous of making yourself known to the auctioneer. There is no need to worry that you have landed yourself with unwanted expense if you feel the need to scratch an itchy ear or sneeze; just raise your arm to catch the auctioneer's eye and soon you will relax and realise you are actually having fun - and do remember to take enough money with you! Lots must be paid for by the end of the day. But do take care: one man came to an auction to buy a bicycle and got so carried away he went home with a pink Cadillac!

Left: Rows of walking stick shaped reinforcement bars are in place for the next stage in the process of widening the Town Bridge in 1938-39. Bank Building, named after Barnard's Bank, is being demolished to make way for the four lane road. When work began on the bridge there was news from the Prime Minister, Neville Chamberlain, that there would be 'peace in our time'. Hitler had signed a treaty saying that he would leave the rest of Czechoslovakia alone, if he were allowed to take over the German speaking Sudeten. Many had serious doubts about his real intentions, but there was a hero who might come to the rescue should he be needed. For the first time the comic strips asked, 'Is it a bird? Is it a 'plane?', and received the answer, 'No! It is Superman!' To the right is the Swan Hotel, which has survived alterations to this area made over the years. Built originally for Francis, the Fifth Duke of Bedford, it did have to sacrifice one of the arches on the riverside of the hotel when the Embankment was widened in the 1860s. The landscaped promenade, which many enjoy today, was once lined with substantial villas on its north bank. Paid for now by the rates and taxes of the people of Bedford, the bridge and road were once maintained by the money gained from toll charges made to anyone wishing to cross. It was not made free of charge until July 1835.

Below: Workers return home after the day shift in the factory c1950. Most of Bedford seems to be on two wheels. Most of them pedal powered. No sign of any of the invading Italian motor scooters yet, but they were growing in popularity. Soon these workers will be able to afford them. Soon the youths of Britain will be identifying themselves as belonging to one of two groups, either 'Mods' or 'Rockers'. Descending on seaside resorts at weekends to do battle. The 'Mods', wearing Italian suits and riding their scooters, and the 'Rockers' in leather outfits on their motorbikes. A far cry from these 'down to earth' hard working Bedfordians. But it is the prosperity, which they bring to the country, that will make such a lifestyle possible. The Festival of Britain, staged on the south bank of the Thames, in London, gave Britain's economy a boost in 1951. Thousands went to see such attractions as 'The Dome of Discovery', where 3-D films were on show. The Pylon, a huge needle shaped structure supported on cables, was one of the attractions. Card cutout models were available in the shops for children to build their own Festival site. Not as good as the real thing, but it stirred the imagination, just as the real thing was intended to stir the attitudes and imaginations of the people and lift them from the austerity of the war.

Above: 'Now let me get this clear in my notes. You say the police box wasn't here when you arrived? Doctor who?' Or maybe the conversation is 'According to my notes it is my turn to drive the car and you are on the bike'. The three-wheeler BSA cars usually had no reverse gear, and it was, therefore, possible to drive them with either a motorcycle licence or a car licence. It was not always easy to set the choke to the right position and get the engine to fire as the cranking handle was turned. Occasionally it would backfire and the handle did not always disengage. But who would not love to own one now, and particularly if your initials are MJ?

Hand signals only. Making a circular motion with the right hand to show that you were about to turn left. The steering on these little cars was very direct and positive. The slightest movement of the steering wheel changed your direction. Whichever one decides to ride the bicycle will have a good view of the world perched high in a 'sit up and beg' position. How we often yearn for the days when the local policeman either walked the beat or rode by on his bike. The Sturmy-Archer gears were operated from the cross bar. Those who remember them will be reminded that it was sometimes necessary to 'back pedal' in order to get the gear to locate.

Above right: The Berkley was a lightweight sports car built onto the glass fibre shell seen in this photograph. Light enough to be propelled at a respectable speed, by a two-stroke twin-cylinder engine. There could be no rust in this appealing little car, and small scratches were invisible on the self-coloured body. It had a cheeky personality and reasonable price tag, which appealed to young people of the time. They were not always in plentiful supply, however, as those produced with left hand drive, as seen in the photograph, were probably in response to the Governments message of the time to 'Export or Die'.

The little sports car suddenly found it had a formidable rival coming onto the market. Designed by Alexander Issigonis, the new Mini was a spacious four seater, with a unique side-mounted 850cc engine. It had character and appeal to equal any of its rivals, and a rally record surpassing most others. Its front wheel drive and innovative suspension meant that it was to be a major success in competition. The Mini starred in films. There was a red one, a white one, and a blue one. They carried out a daring robbery in 'The Italian Job'. They jumped hurdles travelled through pipes and climbed mountains. What else could compare or compete? Film stars and other celebrities decorated them with wicker-patterned doors; they sported stripes and union jacks, they were decorated with painted flowers. They were fashionable. They were winners. The little Berkley was simply born at the wrong time.

A university of the air

According to the Times newspaper: "From outer space to underwater discovery, from nanotechnology to soil science the name of Cranfield University is respected throughout the world". Cranfield degrees are highly sought after in the worlds of industry, commerce, science and defence; but Cranfield graduates receive more than a certificate of achievement when they are presented with their degrees: they become part of history too.

Cranfield University is almost unique: it is one of the few places in the world which can take an aircraft from a design concept, through research and building, all the way through to conducting test flights. Cranfield is the only British university with a working airfield - as well as its own sewage treatment works. It has a world renowned business school and a comprehensive defence capability through the Royal Military College of Science at Shrivenham.

The forerunner of Cranfield University - the College of Aeronautics - was founded in 1946.

During a two-day meeting of the Royal Aeronautical Society in 1943 chaired by the Vice-President Dr Roxbee Cox - who among his many achievements had been Director of Special Projects for the Ministry of Aircraft Production in charge of developing Britain's first Whittle jet engines - it was decided that the current aeronautical education on offer in the UK needed to be revitalised. Also present at the meeting was Sir Roy Feddon: having been granted the meeting's permission to do so, Sir Roy reported to the War Office with the view of persuading the Minister,

Sir Stafford Cripps, that there was a need in the UK for an elite aeronautics school. Sir Roy was successful in his representations and became chairman of a committee formed to advise on creating the College of Aeronautics.

Dr Roxbee Cox, who in 1965 would go on to become Lord Kings Norton of Wotton Underwood, became Cranfield's first Chancellor.

The College of Aeronautics, located at the Royal Air Force Station, Cranfield, would soon become a centre of excellence. The RAF airfield at Cranfield had opened in June 1937 and, in the following month, initially became the base of 62 and 68 Squadrons and their Hawker Hind bi-planes. Hard runways replaced grass

Above: *A group of planes on the airfield in 1946.*
Below: *Cranfield's class of 1946. Roxbee Cox, Roy Fedden and Ernest Relf with board of directors, students and staff.*

in 1940 and soon became the object of enemy attack, being bombed both in August and September of that year. In August 1941 education began at Cranfield when No 51 Operational Training Unit was located there, offering courses to night fighter crews mainly with Blenheims and eventually assuming such importance that Cranfield acquired a satellite at Twinwood airfield, north of Bedford.

At the end of the war, in June 1945, the last war planes flew away. Flying returned within months, however, when the Empire Test Pilots' School transferred to Cranfield from Boscombe Down in November: it would stay there until 1947.

Originally the new college received all its funding directly from the Ministry of Education in the form of an annual grant-in-aid: £3,126 for the period from December 1945 to the end of March 1946, followed by £271,000 for the year ending March 1947 for buildings, staffing and running costs. Professor EF (Ernest) Relf, a distinguished and experienced aerodynamicist from the National Physical Laboratory, was appointed the first Principal. The new 'University of the Air' as it was dubbed, was designed to produce future leaders of industry and research: the first two-year course began in October 1946.

At first only aircraft research and design took place but this eventually led to diversification into other technologies, manufacturing and management through the 1950s and 1960s.

Cranfield College of Aeronautics was renamed Cranfield Institute of Technology (CIT) in 1969 when it was granted the authority to award degrees.

On New Year's Day 1970 a new Vice-Chancellor, Dr Henry Chilver, was appointed. The Chilver years lasted until 1989 and were pivotal to Cranfield's development. The decades after 1970 saw the incorporation of the former National College of Agricultural Engineering at Silsoe into Cranfield University and an academic partnership with the Royal Military College of Science at Shrivenham.

By the time of Chilver's retirement, Cranfield had developed from a college designed for about 100 students specialising only in aeronautics, via aeronautics and management courses in the late 1960s into a degree-awarding chartered institute of technology specialising mainly in post-graduate education in science, engineering, technology and management.

By 1988, only 14 per cent of Cranfield's income came from the government; almost 20 per cent of was

Below: *An aerial view of Cranfield University's Cranfield Campus.* **Insert:** *Cranfield's Charter granted by HM the Queen.*

derived from Cranfield's score of wholly-owned research companies which concentrated on the application of science, while the remainder of income came from industry and commerce.

In 1989 Chilver was succeeded by Professor Frank Hartley (former Principal of the Royal Military College of Science). Under Hartley, Cranfield - one of the smallest higher education institutions in the UK - emerged as the biggest single earner of British industrial research funding. Within five years of his appointment Hartley was able to report that Cranfield was earning fifty per cent more from industry than Imperial College, its nearest rival, and as much as Cambridge and Oxford combined.

1993 saw her Majesty the Queen approve amendments to the Royal Charter renaming CIT as Cranfield University.

Main markets today are as graduate students within the areas of aeronautics, technology, engineering, manufacturing, environmental and medical science and defence, as well as business and management training. To business Cranfield also offers a consultancy service using its wide range of expertise, R&D and specialist facilities.

Excellent teaching standards are supported by relevant research, impressive partnerships and links with industry. Niche subjects and bespoke courses relevant to situations within industry are offered.

The university's mission statement today is to transform world class science, technology, and management expertise into viable practical, environmentally desirable solutions that enhance economic development and the quality of life. Cranfield

University means excellence in military logistics, global security and technology, while within agricultural and environmental circles the Silsoe campus has an enviable reputation for expertise in sustaining the Earth's resources for a rapidly increasing world population.

In the future Cranfield will continue to build on its international reputation for applied research and teaching through developing partnerships to solve problems for industry and commerce and provide career-inspiring opportunities for gifted individuals. Meanwhile, Cranfield will remain Europe's largest academic centre for strategic and applied research, development and design with its leading-edge international reputation virtually guaranteeing career progression for its graduates. Cranfield has certainly come a long way since 1946.

Above left: *Prof. Frank Hartley, Vice-Chancellor.*
Above right: *The award-winning library.*
Right: *Cranfield's Silsoe Campus main building.*

Packing a big punch

Packaging. The modern world would barely function without it. Cardboard cartons and packaging are everywhere, they have become so common that we now find it hard to recall a time when we did not go along to our local fast food outlet and emerge carrying our purchases in well designed and often colourful flat pack cartons - but where did these marvellous products come from? One answer is Bedford.

The internationally known Bedford firm of Colpac Ltd started life as Frank Coleman (Luton) Limited; it had been established by a Luton lay preacher Frank Coleman before the second world war. Whilst Frank Coleman traded, however, Martin Goldman, father of the current MD, joined the armed forces and would spend four years of the war as a prisoner of war in Austria. It was only after the war in 1948 that Martin and his brother Teddy bought the business. Frank Coleman had traded in strawboard for the hat trade and at first the Goldmans continued that business.

After the war the firm traded locally from a small house in Luton manufacturing stitched hat boxes for local hat manufacturers as well as boxes for the dress and engineering trades. In those days most of the firm's customers were based in and around London and it was the transport problem of getting in and out of the capital which forced the business to look for new markets.

Teddy Goldman eventually went off to found another business, Barclay Stuart Plastics, leaving Martin Goldman as sole proprietor.

It was only in the 1950s when the business moved to Dunstable Road in Luton that staff began to be employed. In the early 1960s the firm expanded and started to make rigid boxes for toy and greeting card manufacturers like the Merit Magic Robot quiz game and valentine card makers Fine Arts Carlton.

Below: *Martin Goldman (left) and Neil Goldman.*
Bottom: *The original Frank Coleman factory site is on the bottom centre right.*

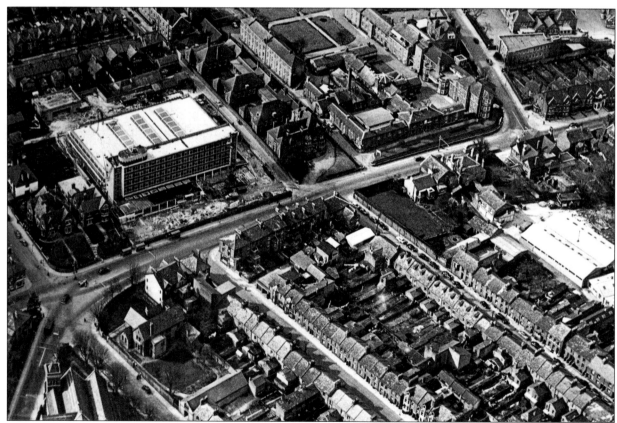

The firm left Luton in 1970 to move to its present building, a 50,000 sq. ft site in Maulden Road, Flitwick. Major capital expenditure was involved, for example a single piece of equipment, a computer aided 'Jagenberg Diana' gluing machine alone cost £350,000.

The business then went into the toy and gift market, manufacturing rigid paper-covered boxes and lids. For several years the firm manufactured hundreds of thousands of boxes for all kinds of industries for example producing the boxes for the board game Trivial Pursuit.

The year 1970 saw a key development: at a fast food fair the firm got its first order from Huckleberry's of Gt. Portland Street, London for cartons, a presage of things to come. Soon the firm was employing a hundred staff. Throughout the mid 1970s the firm began to concentrate on producing printed, folding cartons - what the food industry calls 'disposables' rather than boxes.

Before many years would pass the company would be serving customers all over the UK and abroad, by the early 1990s it was exporting to more than 20 different countries.

In 1993 the firm changed its name to Colpac Ltd, formally adopting a name which had been a brand name already associated with the business for many years and a name readily recognised by people of all nationalities and languages from Berlin to Bermuda. Looking back at his life in 1993 Martin Goldman could reflect with pride, and perhaps a little aston-

ishment how, from a small house in Luton, his firm would one day be selling to such places as far flung as the West Indies, the Far East, the USA, Africa and Europe.

Martin Goldman died in 1994 having been chairman since his retirement; his successor was his son, already the firm's managing director, Neil Goldman.

Colpac now has some 75 employees supplying the catering trade in 36 countries across the globe. The firm still specialises in the design and production of catering disposables - producing a range of sizes and shapes to customers' specifications. The firm's paperboard food packaging products include coffee cup wrappers, popcorn boxes, scoops, cones, and cornets, take way boxes, trays and sleeves, and complete promotions in meal boxes as well as novelty boxes for many other purposes. Today there are only two kinds of people in the world : those who have already used Colpac products - and those who will!

Below left: Food service products in action.
Below right: Colpac site, 1972.

Still providing logistics advice to help British industry lead the world

Nearly fifty years ago a group of enthusiasts founded the Institute of Materials Handling. They had already recognised the immense importance of materials movement and storage to the national economy and that they were involved in an industry that would have rapid growth. In 1968 the Institute of Materials Handling decided to finance a research unit at Cranfield Institute of Technology and out of this evolved the National Materials Handling Centre, with additional support from the equipment manufacturers and Government.

The need, which all these organisations recognised, was for a Centre which would become the focal point for information and advice. It would be a catalyst accelerating the process of industrial recognition. To serve industry effectively it would need to be independent so that its advice could be objective. If industry was to accept its advice it would need to be practical. To maintain its independence and to earn the respect of the industries it served, it would also need to be self-supporting. It was from these beginnings and on this basis that the National Materials Handling Centre was formed in May 1970. The aims of the Centre can be stated simply; firstly to assist British industry to improve its materials management and distribution efficiency; secondly the advancement and dissemination of knowledge of this important part of the national economy. The emphasis is on assisting industry with its problems and it is for this reason that, reacting to industry's requirements, the Centre has developed a wide range of industrial services. From the early days these services covered a wider scope than just materials handling. Indeed, the Centre has always provided advice commercially on all aspects of logistics and the wider supply chain, even though it has only been more recently that these terms have been adopted to describe its work.

The services provided by the National Materials Handling Centre were Logistics Consultancy, Logistics Education and Training, Membership & Information and Logistics Conferences and Seminars. The Centre was set up by the late John Williams as Director.

During the next ten years the National Materials Handling Centre established an enviable reputation for Cranfield, as the leading innovation centre of excellence in logistics, with trend setting conferences training and consultancy advice provided by the Government, as well as to the public and private sectors.

Identifying a need for more substantial training and education in logistics than that provided by the Centre's short courses, NMHC established the first degree courses in logistics and built an extension to their premises on campus to accommodate this initiative. As this activity was clearly academic and not within the Centre's remit, responsibility for the course was transferred to a new University Department called the Cranfield Centre for Logistics and Transportation (CCLT).

On the retirement of John Williams, Ken Firth became Chairman and was responsible for managing the change to a commercially independent organisation from a University Department. For nearly ten years, because of the commercial nature of the Centre's activities it has operated as one of Cranfield University's private companies.

Above: *Warehouse fire test, Cardington Airship sheds - 1970.*

Above: Roger Gutteridge instructs HRH Princess Anne in the craft of rope-making.

During the early 1990s, the expression logistics being more generally used than materials handling, the name Cranfield Logistics Limited was adopted for the consultancy, although the education and information services retained the banner of the National Materials Handling Centre. When Ken Firth in his turn retired, although still located on the University campus, the consultancy has operated under the registered name of Supply Chain Planning Limited. This change of name better reflects the broad activities of the consultancy and the education services have similarly been rebranded as the Logistics Education Centre.

Roger Gutteridge, the current Managing Director, is leading the Consultancy and Education Centre in the 21st century. Roger, himself an NMHC student in the past, is proud of having provided instruction on one occasion to the Princess Royal, although this was much shorter in duration than any NMHC Course!

The logistics consultants advise large and small organisations on supply chain matters as they have for over 30 years, and are particularly proud of the assistance which they provide to third world governments on

Below: The team at a recent Handling Exhibition.

strategy and physical aspects of their supply chains in the food and medical supplies sectors. The Logistics Education Centre had been responsible over the years for training logistics professionals to the highest standards. The courses still set the industry standard, not only in the UK but also in the United States, the Middle East and South East Asia. Recent developments in the best tradition of the National Materials Handling Centre have been the establishment of Supply Chain Strategy Partners Limited, which is leading research into Corporate planning, assessment and development of supply chains and the launch of the unique Simulation Service in the UK and United States for automated warehouses and manufacturing.

Above: A selection of overseas consultancy projects: Top - Tait food warehouse in Taiwan Centre - Hasbro toy manufacturing in Spain Bottom - Medical Supplies operation in Tanzania.

Great walls of fire

What is it that measures 215 x 102.5 x 65mm? No? How about eight and a half inches by four by two and three-quarters? The answer is of course something which we all see everyday of our lives: the common house brick. But there is nothing in the least common about the history of the brick-making industry.

The Hanson Bricks UK factory at Stewartby is part of Hanson group, one of the world's leading building materials companies. Today Hansons has the capacity to provide over three billion bricks each year from its 61 brick factories located in several countries: quite enough bricks to build a wall four feet high around the world.

Brick-making is one of the oldest crafts in the civilised world. The first bricks were made of sun-dried clay and straw: Jericho was built with them 10,000 years ago. Kiln-baking to make the hard durable material we know today was already in use to make the bricks used to build the city of Babylon 8,000 years ago. It was the Romans however who established brick as a major building material in western Europe. It was the Romans who first made bricks in Britain, but the craft was largely forgotten after they left. The industry was not revived until the 13th century.

At that time a brick was known as a 'waltyle' or 'wall-tile', the word 'brick' being first recorded only in 1416. By the reign of Henry VIII in the 16th century English brick-making was sufficiently perfected to make possible brick-built masterpieces such as Hampton Court. The Great Fire of London in 1666 would transform London from a wooden into a brick city and the beauty of the brick built houses built in the reigns of Queen Anne and the Hanoverian kings who followed her set the seal on

Below: Brick-making in the late 1800s.
Bottom: The London Brick Company's Fletton Engineering Department in 1910.

the use of brickwork as a material of dignity and charm.

The Stewartby factory is sited on the belt of Lower Oxford Clay which stretches across England from Yorkshire to the Dorset coast. The uniformity of the clay beds is eminently suited to mechanised brick-making on a large scale.

The discovery in the late 1880s that Lower Oxford Clay almost burns by itself started a small revolution in brick production. Clay for these 'Fletton bricks', named after Fletton near Peterborough, has a high carbon content which provides almost enough fuel to burn on its own. Consequently brick could be produced far more cheaply, which soon had the effect of lowering brick prices generally and increasing demand for them.

Stewartby brickworks is the largest in the Hanson group and the largest in Europe. Although Hanson only acquired the business in 1984 the factory was established in 1898.

Stewartby was formerly known as Wootton Pillinge; it was re-named after the Stewart family, led by its

patriarch Sir Halley Stewart, who had been involved in the business of clay extraction and brick-making from the end of the 19th century.

It was in 1926 that the Stewarts began planning the model village which would be named after them.

Only the very oldest readers of this book will recall the factory as it was before the second world war: one or two may just recall the volunteer fire brigade for example after it was introduced in 1929.

More readers will however remember the various facilities which were provided for workers. By 1935 Stewartby employees were remarkably well provided for with a recently built sports hall, a social club, sports pavilion, and a swimming pool - the latter continuing in use until 1978. Bowling greens and cricket pitches were also laid out.

Perhaps the mundane but rather more recent development will be more easily recalled such as the freightliner-type rail terminal built at Stewartby in 1973 where a large gantry crane could unload containers onto open railway trucks.

Today perhaps 10,000 years after their invention bricks remain as popular as ever in both the developed and developing world. Housing still accounts for the majority of its uses but its widespread availability, proven durability, appearance and relative cheapness have surely secured its future.

Top right: *Tigbourne Court, built in 1900.*
Left: *Brick-making during the second world war.*

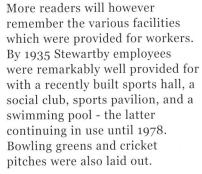

Legal eagles soar in Bedford

The Institute of Legal Executives (ILEX) is the professional body which represents over 22,000 Legal Executives. ILEX is also the leading provider of comprehensive legal education. The Institute is based at Kempston Manor in Kempston.

But what exactly is a Legal Executive, and what is the history behind this prestigious body?

A Legal Executive is a qualified lawyer with at least five years experience of working under the supervision of a solicitor in legal practice or in the legal department of a large company. They have also passed the examinations of ILEX in their area of speciality to the same standard as that required of solicitors. Only Fellows of ILEX can describe themselves as Legal Executives.

Only Fellows of ILEX can describe themselves as Legal Executives

ILEX is the successor to the Solicitors' Managing Clerks Association. That professional body was incorporated back in 1928 though its roots can be traced back to the 19th century. There is a record of a meeting held in the Girdlers' Hall in London in 1892 when some 291 Managing Clerks were in attendance. A solicitor's managing clerk is featured as a person of some importance in Galsworthy's 'Justice' whilst Charles Dickens was for a time a solicitor's clerk.

In 1928 Managing Clerks felt that their branch of the legal profession was in need of regulation and a proper career structure. The Solicitor's Managing Clerks Association was duly incorporated on 26th

Below: Kempston Manor - the headquarters of The Institute of Legal Executives.

Council for the Accreditation of Correspondence Colleges. In the following decades ILEX continued to grow in importance passing such important milestones as being able to represent their client in Magistrate and County Courts and being enabled to act as Commissioners for Oaths.

November 1928 and would serve its members for the next 35 years.

ILEX came into being in 1963 following years of disquiet over an influx of poorly qualified clerks being recruited to solicitors offices and in effect promoting themselves to the status of Managing Clerk though they had neither the experience nor training to enable them to fulfil the duties.

The term Legal Executive came about because of the impossibility of restricting the use of the term Managing Clerk.

On 1st January 1963 ILEX was established with the full support of the Law Society and the Bar Council and the Judiciary. Its promoters were determined that those who would be admitted to their branch of the legal profession should be properly trained.

A formal scheme of education was adopted with examinations at two levels: the first at 'A' level standard, the second made up of three papers set at degree level. In his chosen field of law the Legal Executive would be as well qualified as a solicitor.

To help achieve its educational aims and recognising the need for good distance learning courses to help aspiring Legal Executives to qualify the ILEX Tutorial College (ITC) was established in June 1983. By the following year the ITC had been awarded a certificate of accreditation by the

By 1999 ILEX was recognised as an authorised body for awarding litigation rights to suitably qualified members by the Access to Justice Act which will enable Legal Executives in the future to set up in the High Street under their own names.

Today the Institute of Legal Executives is an accepted partner in the legal life of the United Kingdom. It is not a trade union but is the body responsible for regulating the professional life of its members and for providing a system of proper training.

Membership of the Institute now stands in excess of 22,000 including members from as far afield as Bermuda and Hong Kong. There are ILEX branches throughout England and Wales. In 1998 Lord Woolf, Master of the Rolls at that time and subsequently Lord Chief Justice, accepted the honorary Vice Presidency of ILEX.

The status and professionalism of the Legal Executive has certainly come a long way since that far off day in 1892 when the founders of the profession met in London's Girdlers' hall to form their first Association; little could they have imagined what the seeds they were planting would eventually grow into.

Above left: *A recent Graduation Ceremony in Bedford Corn Exchange.* ***Above right:*** *A Legal Executive at work.*

Silver Street in 1941 and
rationing was just
beginning to bite

Acknowledgments

The publishers would like to thank
Richard Wildman for his help in the course of research and proof-reading.
Bedfordshire and Luton Archives and Records Service. Most of the editorial
images contained in this book were from the Bedford County Record Office
Collection, original photographs from Beds. County Press.

Thanks are also due to
John Thornton who penned the editorial text
and Steve Ainsworth for his copywriting skills